ROAD BOSS

AC/DC, ANDY GIBB, ANDY WILLIAMS, ANNE MURRAY, ANTHONY QU[illegible] ARTHUR FOGEL,
BACHMAN-TURNER OVERDRIVE (BTO), BAD CO[illegible]E
BOYS, THE BEACH BOYS, THE BEATLES, BI[illegible],
BILL COSBY, BILL MEDLEY, BLACK SABBATH, THE [illegible],
BOB MARLEY, BOB SEGER, BOBBY CURTOLA, B[illegible]Y,
BON JOVI, BRENDA LEE, BRUCE WILLIS, BUDDY KNOX, BRYAN ADAMS, CARL PERKINS, CARL WILSON, CARLOS SANTANA,
CHAR[illegible]ER, CHUCK BERRY,
CHUCK N[illegible]LS AND NASH (CSN), DAVID
BOW[illegible] DAVID FISHOF, DEL
SHANNON, DENZEL WASHINGTON, DIANA ROSS, DIRTY DANCING TOUR, DIONNE
WARWICK, DIZZY GILLE[illegible]NING,
DR. HOOK, EAGLES, EDDIE MONEY, [illegible]N, ERIC
CLAPTON, THE EVERLY BROTHERS, [illegible]TRICAL
BAND, FOREIGNER, FRANK ZAPPA, GATLIN BROTHERS, GENESIS, GEORGE FOX, GEORGE MICHAEL, GERRY LEE LEWIS, GENE
PITNEY, GEORGIA SATELLITES, GORDON LIGHTFOOT, GRAND FUNK RAILROAD, THE GRATEFUL
DEAD, THE GUESS WHO, HANK WILLIAMS JR., HARRY BELAFONTE,
HUEY LEWIS, IGGY POP, IRON MAIDEN, IRVING AZOFF, JACKIE MASON, JANIS JOPLIN, JAMES BROWN, JERRY LEE
LEWIS, JETHRO TULL, JIM GORDON, JIMMY CONNORS, JOEL GREY, JOE COCKER, JOHN
DENVER, JOHN ENTWISTLE, JOHN MCENROE, JOHN MELLENCAMP, JOHNNY AND SANTO, JUDAS PRIEST, KEITH RICHARDS,
KENNY LOGGINS, KISS, LED ZEPPELIN, LENNY KRAVITZ, LESLIE WEST, LITTLE RICHARD, LOS LOBOS, LYNYRD SKYNYRD,
MARK FARNER, MARTHA AND THE VANDELLAS, MEN AT WORK, MICHAEL JACKSON, MICHAEL J. FOX,
MICHELLE WRIGHT, MICK JAGGER, MICKEY ROONEY, MITCH RYDER
AND THE DETROIT WHEELS, MOLLY HATCHET, MÖTLEY CRÜE,
MOUNTAIN, MR. T, NANA MOUSKOURI, NATALIE COLE, NEIL YOUNG, THE
NEVILLE BROTHERS, NEW KIDS ON THE BLOCK, NINE INCH NAILS, NITTY GRITTY DIRT BAND, THE NYLONS,
THE OAK RIDGE BOYS, PAUL MCCARTNEY, PAUL REVERE AND THE RAIDERS, PEGGY
LEE, PETE TOWNSHEND, PETER NOONE (HERMAN'S HERMITS), PETER, PAUL AND MARY,
PETER TOSH, POISON, PRINCE, RARE EARTH, RAVI SHANKAR,
RAY CHARLES, RIGHTEOUS BROTHERS, RICHARD HARRIS, RICKIE LEE JONES, RICKY
NELSON, RICKY VAN SHELTON, RINGO STARR, ROBERT GOULET,
ROBERT PALMER, ROBERT PLANT, RODNEY DANGERFIELD, ROGER DALTREY,
ROGER MCGUINN, THE ROLLING STONES, RON WOOD, RONNIE SPECTOR,
ROSEMARY CLOONEY, ROY ORBISON, SAM CAHN, SASS JORDAN, SHA NA NA, SHARON, LOIS & BRAM, SHEP
GORDON, SIMON & GARFUNKEL, STEPPENWOLF, STEVIE WONDER, STRAY CATS,
TAMMI WYNETTE, TED NUGENT, THE ANIMALS, THE BAND, THE CONTOURS,
THE DOOBIE BROTHERS, THE GRATEFUL DEAD, THE GUESS WHO, THE JACKSONS, THE MOODY
BLUES, THE MONKEES, THE POLICE, THE RAMONES,
THE RASCALS, THE ROLLING STONES, THE TEMPTATIONS, THE WHO, TIM
CONWAY, TINA TURNER, TOM JONES, TRAVIS TRITT, UB40, U2, VAN HALEN, VINCE GILL, WAYNE
GRETZKY, WILLIE NELSON, YUL BRYNNER, ZZ TOP

ROAD BOSS

UNTOLD STORIES FROM ENTERTAINMENT'S ULTIMATE TOUR MANAGER

MARTY KRAMER

WITH

David Wolinsky

mosaicPRESS

Library and Archives Canada Cataloguing in Publication

Library and Archives Canada Cataloguing in Publication

Title: Road boss: untold stories from entertainment's ultimate tour manager / Marty Kramer; with David Wolinsky.

Names: Kramer, Marty, author. | Wolinsky, David (Retired lawyer), author.

Identifiers: Canadiana (print) 20250184672 | Canadiana (ebook) 20250185911

ISBN 9781771618083 (softcover) | ISBN 9781771618090 (PDF) |
ISBN 9781771618106 (EPUB) | ISBN 9781771618113 (Kindle)

Subjects: LCSH: Kramer, Marty. | LCSH: Concert agents—Canada—Biography. | LCSH: Road crews (Concert tours)—Canada—Biography. | LCGFT: Autobiographies.

Classification: LCC ML429.K89 A3 2025 | DDC 781.64092—dc23

Published by Mosaic Press, Oakville, Ontario, Canada, 2025.

MOSAIC PRESS, Publishers
www.Mosaic-Press.com

Cover Design: Amy Land

ONTARIO CREATES

Funded by the Government of Canada
Financé par le gouvernement du Canada

Canada

MOSAIC PRESS
1252 Speers Road, Units 1 & 2, Oakville, Ontario, L6L 2X4 (905) 825-2130
info@mosaic-press.com • www.mosaic-press.com

DISCLAIMER

THIS IS A WORK OF NON-FICTION. AS FAR AS MY STORIES ARE CONCERNED, THEY'RE ALL TRUE, AND I HAVE THE PICTURES, THE FILMS, THE VIDEOS, THE DOCUMENTS, AND THE MEMORABILIA TO BACK THEM UP. SO BUCKLE UP, BUTTERCUP. I'M ABOUT TO TELL YOU EVERYTHING ABOUT ROCK 'N' ROLL YOU DIDN'T KNOW BUT WANTED TO.

CONTENTS

VI Stories Behind the Stories

VII Odds and Ends

VIII Yes, Virginia, There May Be No Santa Claus, But There Is Life After Rock 'n' Roll

As a man sow, shall he reap
And I know that talk is cheap
But the harder the battle
The sweeter the victory

—Bob Marley

FOREWORD

Let's say you're visiting New York, Los Angeles, or London, and by sheer chance, you find yourself in the same restaurant as your favorite singer, comedian, or movie star.

Gathering your courage, you approach the celebrity and ask for an autograph or, better yet, a selfie. A moment to remember and cherish, right?

Now imagine you're Marty Kramer, a poor Jewish kid from the north end of Winnipeg who, by sheer chance, gets to meet not one or two but dozens of the biggest names in show business. Not just meet them—actually work for them.

The titles they confer on him may vary—road manager, fixer, concert promoter—but the titles are irrelevant. The point is, that Marty occupies the catbird seat in the world of entertainment.

Ringo Starr, Neil Young, Frank Sinatra, Roy Orbison, Tina Turner, Denzel Washington, Jackie Mason, Harry Belafonte, Rodney Dangerfield, David Copperfield, Eddie Murphy, Bruce Willis—Marty worked for them all. And the list is endless.

So this is Marty's story, accompanied by the interwoven memories of his long-time friend and lawyer, David Wolinsky.

Oh, and I lied about calling it sheer chance. In Marty's case, it wasn't chance at all.

Okay, maybe the first time, when he was recruited to stand in the wings of a Led Zeppelin performance and, at the right moment, walk on stage to hand a guitar to Jimmy Page.

But after that, it was something else—a magical combination of chutzpah, street smarts, resourcefulness, and likeability. And the stars recognized that.

Marty was cheerful. Marty was clever. Marty got things done. (Example: Frank Sinatra needs to watch CNN in his dressing room—

Marty persuades technicians to rewire an entire arena.) Marty was trustworthy. He kept his mouth shut about things that required discretion.

So this is not a tell-all book. There are no sordid tales of debauchery. First and foremost, Marty's a mensch.

Instead, this is a book about Marty's charmed, serendipitous life—even he sometimes has trouble believing it—the extraordinary cast of characters he met, and what he learned about them.

It's a great ride. I hope you enjoy it as much as I did.

Michael Posner
October 2024

PREFACE

My name is Martin Kramer. Some people call me Marty. And a few old friends from back in the *shtetl* (village) call me by my Hebrew name Moishe. For most of my life, however, the vast majority have always just called me Kramer. Just Kramer. Long before the other Kramer from *Seinfeld*. So please, just call me Kramer.

Truth be told, my birth name really isn't Kramer. I was an orphan and spent my first couple of years in an orphanage until I was adopted. I didn't learn my real name or the fact that I had a couple of sisters until a few years ago. Having said all of that, though, my name really won't mean anything to most of you who will never have heard of me or have any idea just who the hell I am. But if you love rock 'n' roll or if you love music generally, I'm somebody you want to know. I've been everywhere you wish you could have been, known all the people you wish you had known, and have all the stories you wish you could tell.

So, how does an orphan from a small city in the Midwest that most of you have likely never heard of, who never knew his biological parents, and left school after Grade 10, manage to make a living interacting with some of the biggest celebrities in the world? I'm talking about more than 25 groups or individuals who, at one time or another, were number one in the world in their respective field, and 56 of *Rolling Stone* magazine's 100 greatest artists of the past 100 years.

For some of these, I was either a tour or road manager, or sometimes both. For others, I was a personal manager or representative. And for still more, I was the concert production manager. But on more occasions than I can recall, I was also what in politics is referred to as a body man. In U.S. political jargon, that's a civilian personal assistant who accompanies a politician virtually everywhere. The role of the body man is to be on hand to offer any necessary assistance, including arranging lodging, managing interactions with the media, the public, and family, coordinating meals, and conducting personal briefings.

When they did a documentary on my life a few years ago, it was called *Get Marty*, because in the industry, the word was if you needed anything done, involving production, an artist, manager, or tradesperson, you should "Get Marty." When I left Toronto to move to the coast, David Bluestein, head of Canada's The Agency, gave me a one-line letter of reference that read, "To Whom It May Concern. Hire Kramer now."

So, in the great maze we call life, I served as the body man for visiting celebrities of all stripes. I'm talking about the Beatles and Ringo Starr, Frank Sinatra, Dean Martin, Sammy Davis Jr., Neil Young, The Who, The Rolling Stones, Bob Dylan, Simon and Garfunkel, The Monkees, Led Zeppelin, and The Eagles, just to scratch the surface. And along the way, a few other non-music giants such as President Bill Clinton, Wayne Gretzky, Bruce Willis, Rodney Dangerfield, Jackie Mason, and Yul Brynner also found their way into my world.

But back to the $64,000 question of how I accomplished this. My motto has always been "No excuses. Get the job done and keep a record." As the great Freddie Mercury said "Darling, my attitude is 'Fuck it.' I'm doing everything with everybody."

Well, I did everything with everybody…and lived to tell about it.

1
IN THE BEGINNING

1

THE ARTIST COMES FIRST

It was the late 1960s, and the British Invasion was at its peak. The three biggest bands in the world were The Beatles, The Rolling Stones, and Led Zeppelin. Two of the three—the Stones and Led Zeppelin—had scheduled concerts in my hometown. We're talking about the original Rolling Stones lineup: Mick Jagger, Keith Richards, Brian Jones, Charlie Watts, and Bill Wyman, and the original Led Zeppelin: Jimmy Page, Robert Plant, John Paul Jones, and John Bonham.

As a young kid, I knew that the world of music was where I wanted to be. I associated with all the musicians in town, helping with bookings, looking after equipment, and doing all the things they were too busy to do. Even in those early days, I had two rules: (1) The artist comes first, and (2) Always take care of business. Through this, I got to know most of the local players on the music scene.

When the concert dates were announced, I knew there was no way I could afford tickets. I went to the promoter, whom I knew, and told him I wanted to work the shows for free. He knew I was reliable, so he hired me. His instructions were clear: "You look after the boys—the Stones and Zeppelin. Get them whatever they need. Get them to and from the stage. Whatever they want or need, take care of it. I don't want to be bothered."

The first concert was The Rolling Stones, and everything went smoothly. Led Zeppelin was next. Just before taking them to the stage, the production manager came to me and said, "Jimmy Page needs a couple of guitars handed to him during the performance. The guy who usually does it has to be on the other side of the stage, so I need you to do it."

I smiled and said, "No problem." There was a problem, though—I couldn't pick Jimmy Page out of a lineup if it had only two people: him and Jimmy Olsen from the Superman comics. Rather than panicking, I said, "I'm a big fan of the guys, but I've never seen them in concert before. Could you point out where Jimmy will be standing so I can position myself accordingly?"

He took me to the stage and pointed out the setup: "Robert Plant, the lead singer, is there. Bonham on drums is there. John Paul Jones on bass is there. And Jimmy is over here. Stand beside the amp and hand him the guitars when he signals you."

And that's what I did. I took one from him and gave him another. And that was the start of my career.

Lesson number one: Every tour or road manager thinks their artist is the greatest in the world. Telling them you have no idea who their artist is won't instill much confidence. So, work around it. That's why word quickly spread: If you wanted things done properly, you got Marty. In the industry, it became known that hiring Marty Kramer meant no excuses, no worries—everything would be looked after. And if something unexpected happened, I'd fix it rather than come looking for help.

Looking after the Stones and Zeppelin led to gigs as tour or road manager for several local bands that had made it big internationally. From there, my work just kept expanding.

2

COLLECT MORE THAN MEMORIES

The Rolling Stones concert was also the start of my second career. As a poor kid, I had almost nothing, so I learned to appreciate something. Watching my friends collect and trade baseball and football cards, which I couldn't afford to do, helped me understand the value of collecting things. I also grasped that what wasn't valuable today might become very valuable tomorrow.

Once I started drawing a salary, I committed 25% of whatever I made to acquiring things that would someday be valuable. I was able to acquire many of these items, such as pictures, posters, or other memorabilia related to the artists for whom I was working for little to nothing. I made it my cardinal rule to get anything and everything signed and personalized by these artists along the way. In addition to memorabilia, however, I have also acquired tens of thousands of 45s, albums, CDs, DVDs, films, videos, books, articles, posters, and everything else imaginable related to various musical artists, concentrating on only those items that I knew would greatly increase in value.

As well, I expanded my field to include all the other collectibles, including trading cards, comics, pinball machines, Wurlitzers, toys, and so on, to the point where I now have almost 20,000 square feet of these collectibles, all catalogued and increasing in value day by day. I believe I have more valuable collectibles of most artists than they have themselves.

It all started with Mick Jagger. I had borrowed a Polaroid camera from a friend before I came to work that day with the intention of getting some pictures of the band. I went to the dressing room to let the guys know they would be going on shortly, and figured that would be the best time to get a picture. Unfortunately, they were all busy doing their own thing. I realized that there was no way I could get the band together for a photo, so I just asked Mick if it would be alright to take a picture of him. He was a gentleman, of course, and said, "By all means."

These were the days when after you took a Polaroid, you had to let it dry for about a minute before you applied a coating to preserve it. Right after I took the picture, there was a knock at the door telling us it was time to get the band to the stage. There was no time to coat the picture, and I wasn't going to leave it in the dressing room. It was still moist, and putting it in my pocket would just ensure it was covered with lint, so I tucked it into my sock around my ankle and took the band to the stage. I suppose I could have tucked it into the back of my underwear, but I figured in case it stuck to my skin, it would be easier to explain a picture of Mick on my ankle than on my keister.

After the performance, I took the band back to the dressing room and went to remove the photo, and indeed found it was stuck to my ankle. I managed to peel it off, and fortunately, it was only ruined around the edges—the rest of the picture was fine.

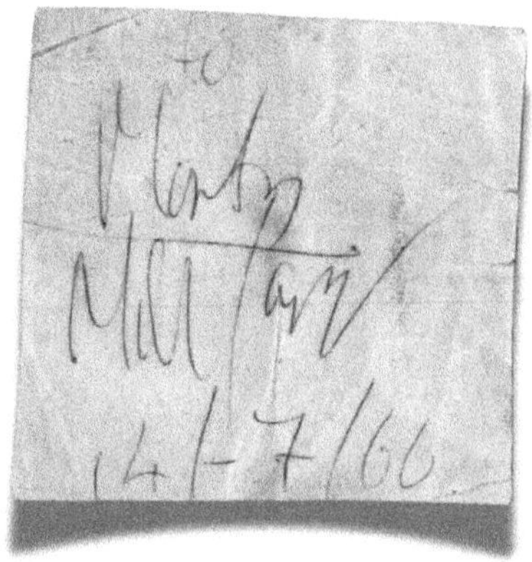

I got Mick to sign it for me, and then I coated it, and that was the start of my collection. I suppose if I were more sentimental, I would have had a small picture of Mick tattooed on my ankle, but I think I read somewhere something about how Jews aren't supposed to get tattoos, especially Jews who were afraid of needles.

That initial meeting with the Stones was more than just the start of my collecting career. It was also a lesson. I had the privilege of working their American Tour in 1981, their Voodoo Lounge Tour in 1994, and their Bridge to Babylon Tour in 1998, and the only other occasion I asked for some signed memorabilia was in December 1994. Although the promoter and I were planning on visiting the band after the show at the Four Seasons where he was planning on presenting them with a thank-you gift, I got them to sign the record slick you see on the opposite page (the promo slick they put in stores to sell the album) right after I picked them up at the airport. He who hesitates is not only lost, he winds up peeling things off his body.

I'm confident there is no other record slick anywhere signed by all four Stones, so this is exceptionally rare.

3

BOOZE AND BUSINESS DON'T MIX (AT LEAST FOR ME)

Busted flat in Nowhereville, driving from a train
Feeling near as faded as my jeans
Janis nursed a bottle of some Southern Comfort booze
Almost put an end to all my dreams

Early in my career, before I looked after a national tour, let alone an international one, *The Festival Express* was coming to our town, and I was hired as the stage manager. *The Festival Express* was a 1970 train tour of some of North America's most popular rock artists and included The Grateful Dead, Janis Joplin, Delaney and Bonnie, The Band, Buddy Guy, Mountain. and Ian & Sylvia's Great Speckled Bird. Rather than flying into each city, they had chartered a 12-car train. There were five sleeping cars, two lounge cars, two flat cars, one baggage car, one dining car, and a staff car.

In those days, we'd set the stage for one act, and while that act was performing, we'd set the stage for another act on a mobile riser and then roll it out, which meant we were always busy working behind the scenes. Rather than all the bands showing up at one time, we'd have to run back and forth to where the train was parked near the station to get them. So, for example, a band would perform, and then they'd go back to the train, and the gear would follow. Then the next band would leave the train. There was a constant shuttle going on. When it was time to take Janis Joplin to the stadium, she declined a car pointed right at me and said, "I want to go in the truck with that guy." I had the truck because I was taking some gear back to the stadium, so she ended up riding up front with me in my Budget Rent-a-Truck. To my horror, as soon as she got in, a bottle of Southern Comfort materialized, and she started drinking from it.

To get to the stadium where the bands were performing, we had to drive through the main street of our town. As we drove, Janis was sitting beside me, swigging from her bottle. Suddenly, she rolled down her window, leaned out, and started waving the bottle around and shouting, "Follow us to the stadium for the show. Follow us to the arena for the show."

People saw her and started screaming, "It's Janis Joplin, it's Janis Joplin." Suddenly, I'm the Pied Piper. People were running beside my truck, waving and shouting, and a growing line of cars was forming behind us with people hanging out their windows, shouting and honking their horns. Now, at that time, having an open bottle of liquor in your car was a criminal offence and could get you thrown in jail. This might not be a big deal for a star, but for Joe Citizen, aka me, it could be a career changer. And I'm leading a parade down Main Street with the first lady of rock 'n' roll hanging out the passenger window, waving a bottle of booze and screaming, "Follow us. Follow us."

I learned a valuable lesson that day. Booze and drugs were an integral part of the music industry. Less than three months later, Janis died from a heroin overdose compounded by alcohol. If I ever hoped for a life in the music business outside the city limits of Nowhere, drugs and booze couldn't be part of the equation.

4

YOU GET THE PICTURE

One of the basic tenets of my life has been, "Always keep your word." When you say you will do something and don't do it, you teach others that you cannot be trusted.

It was the mid-sixties, with the British Invasion underway. I received a call from my buddy, local DJ Daryl Birmingham. Daryl said, "Pack your bag, Marty. You're going to see the Beatles." All I could utter was "I am?" "Yes, you are," Daryl said, "They're doing a concert in Minneapolis and representatives from a dozen radio stations in surrounding towns have been invited for a meet and greet and to see the concert, and you're going to be my technical assistant."

Even at that young age, I recognized the need for memorabilia, so I called my uncle, who owned a camera store, and arranged to borrow a camera for the occasion. He told me to come down and take what I wanted and threw in rolls of black and white and color film. And then we were off.

We got to the arena, and it was mayhem. We received our credentials and proceeded to the press room. There were other people from around a dozen stations from places like Fargo, Grand Forks, Duluth, and some small towns in Wisconsin. Shortly thereafter, one of the Beatles' staff came in and introduced himself. He told us that he would be taking us in to meet the guys, we would each be allowed a five-minute interview, and if we wanted, to take three pictures. And of course, we would receive tickets to the show. Daryl conducted his interview, and then I took my pictures. I'm not sure why, but I used color films.

After this was done, we left to watch the show. I'd like to say it was one of their best, but John Lennon was suffering from laryngitis and Paul and George had to carry much of the singing. Still, the Beatles were never less than great.

When I got back home, I developed the pictures and tucked them away. Over the years, I remained close with Darryl B., who gained national prominence across the nation as the DJ's DJ until he went to rock and roll heaven in 2001.

Fast forward to 1995. We were getting ready to leave for the *Ringo Starr All-Starr Band Tour*, and Ritchie and I were just sitting around chatting. I said, "I'm not sure if you remember, but we met around 30 years ago when you played Minneapolis. John was suffering from laryngitis at the time. We interviewed you, and I took some great color photos of the band." He asked if I still had them, and I replied that of course, I did. He told me he was putting out a book of pictures shortly and would love to include them. I gave him my word that he would have the pictures as soon as we got back from the tour. When we got back, however, I was unable to find them.

A few years after the end of the tour, Ritchie was playing in Seattle, so I went to see the show and say hello. We weren't five minutes into the conversation before Ritchie said, "So Mahrty, did you find the pictures?" Sadly, I had to tell him I still had not.

Fast forward to today. I just finished reading Ritchie's new book, *Another Day in the Life*, a wonderful collection of his pictures and stories, and was reminded of my unfulfilled promise. For the past year, in preparation for the publication of my book, I've been going through literally hundreds of thousands of records, CDs, DVDs, tapes, pictures, cards, posters, contracts, and other memorabilia. With this promise in mind, I embarked on a renewed search, and in the back of one of the storage rooms beneath a dozen boxes, I found a small, old filing cabinet. Instinctively, before I even opened the drawer, I knew I had found the missing pictures. And sure enough, at the back of the drawer in a manila envelope, there they were. I immediately sent them off to Ritchie with a short note of apology for the delay.

Promises made, promises kept. It may have taken me 27 years, but at least one less sin for which to atone.

5

GUESS WHO STARTED IT ALL

I would be remiss if I failed to mention Canada's greatest gift to the world of music, The Guess Who. Yes, there were Rush, Celine Dion, Bryan Adams, The Barenaked Ladies, and numerous other wonderful Canadian artists, but The Guess Who and their principal founders, Randy Bachman and Burton Cummings, started it all.

Their international success started in 1969 with the release of their album *Wheatfield Soul* and the single "These Eyes," which was their first top-ten hit and went gold with over a million records sold. This was followed later in the year with *Canned Wheat* and the hits "Laughing," "Undone," and "No Time." They followed this in 1970 with the release of the album *American Woman,* and the single of the same name rose to number one on the charts, the first Canadian group to ever achieve that status. Randy Bachman left the group that year, and there were several personnel changes over the next four years, but the band continued to flourish. In late 1970, they were invited by Richard Nixon to perform at the White House, which they did. The group disbanded in 1974, but over the next 30 years reunited for reunion tours on several occasions. Burton Cummings pursued a hugely successful solo career from 1975 to date and continues to be in huge demand. As well, Cummings and Bachman reunited on several occasions to perform as Bachman Cummings.

After leaving the Guess Who, Bachman formed his own band, Brave Belt, which ultimately evolved into Bachman-Turner Overdrive (BTO) with Randy, C.F. (Fred) Turner, and Randy's brothers Robbie and Tim. BTO achieved international success and became the number-one band in the world with their international hits "You Ain't Seen Nothing Yet" and "Takin' Care of Business." Whereas The Guess Who relied more on a soft rock influence, BTO, with C.F. Turner's gruff, growly voice, made the band, as Robby Bachman put it, "A working man's kind of rock and roll." This probably explained why, for many years, they were the headliners for the half a million bikers who gathered annually in Sturgis, South Dakota, for the bikers' rally where BTO's "Let It Ride" and "Roll on Down the Highway" were anthems. Randy left the band in 1977, and although there were several reunions over the subsequent years, Randy mostly pursued a highly successful individual career, which he continues to this date, always highly in demand.

In addition to being consummate artists, it was the music of Cummings and Bachman that has made such an impact over the years. You would be hard-pressed to go to any city in North America and not hear some of their songs being played on the radio, on television, in a store, or on an elevator. "American Woman" was covered by Lenny Kravitz in 1999 to great success, and the song has been utilized in numerous films and television shows as well as covered by numerous other artists. Like "American Woman," "Takin' Care of Business" was utilized in numerous major films and television shows and was reportedly the most licensed song in Sony Music's catalog. Numerous other songs by Bachman and Cummings have made their catalogs hugely successful over the years.

For more than forty years, I was tour/road or production manager for The Guess Who, Bachman Turner Overdrive, Randy Bachman, and Burton Cummings. More importantly, for more years than that, I have been blessed to call Randy Bachman and Burton Cummings my friends. And no matter what else I may be involved with, if either one of them calls and says he needs me, I will always be there.

PRINCE
17 NOV 1988
LOVESEXY '88
BUILDING
GUEST PASS
The JACKSONS
VICTORY TOUR '84
SPECIAL
Lower Press
A
2
LEGENDS OF
ROCK AND ROLL
VAN HALEN
FACILITY PASS
NAZARETH
FACILITY PASS
U2 ZOO TV TOUR
JETHRO TULL
PRO
TORONTO
ALL ACCESS
ERIC CLAPTON
TOUR '88
VAN
/HOUSE/

6

NOT ALL STARS ARE DIVAS

I could probably write an entire book about my travels with Ringo Starr, but out of respect for his concern with privacy, I am going to limit it mostly to this chapter. I'm hopeful that he won't mind the stories that I tell, as they only underline what an exceptional, decent, multitalented, and down-to-earth man he is.

My regard for the great Ringo Starr began when he said, "Maahrteee (it's how he pronounced my name with a lovely English accent), my friends all call me Ritchie. You'll call me Ritchie." Throughout all our travels, he was always accessible to me, without any formalities, notice, or other impediments so many superstars place in the way of people who work for them. As far as Ritchie was concerned, you were working *with* him, not *for* him, and should be accorded that respect.

It was the 1995 *Ringo Starr and His All-Starr Band Tour*, and we were playing Pittsburgh. On many occasions, the local promoter of the event would ask to take pictures with Ritchie, and he would always oblige. On some occasions, the promoter might also want to do something to honor Ritchie, and if it was something relatively private, once again, Ritchie would be there.

On this occasion, the local promoter came to me and said that in honor of Ritchie coming to Pittsburgh, he'd like to present him with an award honoring him for his contributions to the music industry. I asked how many people would be involved, and he said just a couple. I said, "Give me a few minutes. I'll go and set it up."

I went to Ritchie's trailer and explained what I'd been told. He agreed, and I brought him to the hospitality tent. As we walked in, we were greeted by the promoter and around 150 other guests. I put out a hand to stop Ritchie, but he merely nodded his head, indicating it was okay, and smiled as he was presented with a beautiful plaque. Afterward, I went to apologize to Ritchie, but he merely smiled and said, "It happens. Not to worry." Once burned, twice shy. I made certain that it never happened again.

Shortly thereafter, Ritchie's wife, Barbara, came to me and said, "This plaque is too big for us to carry in our luggage. Can you put it in your production box, and we'll get it at the end of the tour?" I replied that, of course, I'd be happy to do so. I promptly put it in my production box and then forgot about it. When we arrived in Las Vegas for the last couple of dates, a family emergency arose, and we had to cancel the remaining concert dates so that Ritchie could fly to Boston.

After arranging for the other band members to get home and clearing up other matters related to the tour's end, including air freighting my production box home, I headed home. When it arrived, I started to unpack it, and when I got to the bottom drawer, which was the largest, I found the plaque. I had totally forgotten about it, and I knew I had to get it to Ritchie right away with a note, thanking him for everything during the tour. Before doing this, however, I wanted to make sure it was still pristine and that no damage had occurred during transit. I took the plaque out of its sleeve, examined the front, and then turned it over and saw it had been inscribed: "Marty. This is for you. WOW. Ringo/1995."

If I were asked to define star quality, I would say it is not only possessing rare talent or being willing to share it, it's having the decency and awareness of the people around you to the extent that you recognize that, although they might not be able to share the rarefied stratosphere you dwell in, their lives are equally meaningful and should be encouraged and acknowledged. Ritchie was the embodiment of this. He understood that I was a collector and knew that the plaque would be more meaningful to me than to him.

I only recently learned of Ritchie's investiture as a Knight Bachelor and of course, was thrilled for him. There is nobody more deserving or more beloved, both for his artistry and his community and charitable works. Still, a part of me expects that, although honored, he wouldn't be totally comfortable with it. Despite his remarkable accomplishments, what makes him so exceptional is that he's always remained one of us.

DiCesare Engler
Congratulates
RINGO STARR
IN RECOGNITION OF
YOUR ENDLESS CONTRIBUTIONS
TO THE MUSIC INDUSTRY
AUGUST 1 1995
I. C. LIGHT AMPHITHEATRE
PITTSBURGH, PENNSYLVANIA

7

LIKE A ROLLING STONE, OR MORE CORRECTLY LIKE A STONE ROLLING ACROSS THE DECADES

It was the spring of the early sixties, and I was just a teenager. The Jewish holiday of Passover had arrived. Most families held what are called Seders, Passover dinners, which generally were a large gathering of the entire family as well as friends and often strangers who had nowhere else to go.

We generally had a very small Seder. My adoptive parents were poor, so we never had a lot of people at our house. On this occasion, earlier in the day, my best friend with whom I would hang out all the time said, "When your Seder is over, come over to my house and we'll go to the pool hall and have a kibitz." He called just as we finished our Seder and said, "Come on over, we've got some relatives in from out of town. We're going to have dessert. Come over for dessert now, and then we'll go play some pool."

Most of the Jews lived in the north end of our city, in what I call the shtetl, the village, and most lived within a few blocks of one another. I walked into the house and my friend introduced me, saying, "This is my best friend, Marty Kramer. He's going to have dessert with us." Then his mother said, "Marty, I'd like you to meet Mr. and Mrs. Zimmerman and their son Robert." I knew from nothing. There were two older folks and a younger guy sitting there, the kid's quiet, curly, Brillo kind of hair. I said, "Pleased to meet you." We had dessert, and then my friend and I left. I asked him who the kid with the funny hair was, and he said, "It's my first cousin. They drove in from Hibbing, Minnesota. He's some kind of folk singer."

A few years later, when my friend and I were talking, he mentioned his cousin and how he was doing very well as a folk singer. I said, "I've never heard of a singer named Robert Zimmerman." He said, "No, he changed his name. To Bob Dylan."

It was twenty-some years later, and we'd just finished the U.S. leg of *The Guess Who Reunion Tour*. Shep Gordon, the tour manager, had offered Burton and me his beach house in Maui for a month, and we decided to take him up on it, take the month off, and go and relax. Burton wanted to stop in L.A. at his house first to regroup, and then we'd head off to Maui.

We were in the Minneapolis airport waiting for our flight to L.A. I looked and two benches over there was Bob Dylan. I had just read the recent edition of *Rolling Stone,* whose cover story featured Bob Dylan's 19th studio album, *Slow Train Coming*. I went over to the newsstand and picked up a copy of the magazine and a marker pen, and then I went over and introduced myself. I said, "I manage Burton Cummings. We recognized you. I hope I'm not disrupting anything you're doing."

He said, "No."I said, "I just got a copy of the *Rolling Stone*. I'm a big fan. I'd love you to sign it. I'm a collector." I opened it up to the article on him, and he signed the whole page. I put it away.

I thanked him and then I said, "By the way, where are you going?" He said, "L.A." I said, "We're going to L.A. as well." He said, "I'm having trouble trying to arrange for a limo in L.A.," to which I responded, "We have a limo at the airport to take us to Burton's place in Sherman Oaks. You're welcome to share it with us." He said, "Won't that be an inconvenience?" and I replied, "Absolutely not. We'll go from the airport to Sherman Oaks, and then the limo will drop you off wherever you want to go. It's already paid for, so we might as well make use of it." We all flew together first class to L.A.; our limo dropped us off, and I instructed the driver to take him wherever he wanted to go.

The next time I saw him was some twenty years later. I was doing a show for Perryscope Concerts starring Dylan. At the back of the facility, there was a basketball hoop, and the crew was tossing around the ball. I had my production office at the facility, and I was there working the show. I saw Dylan standing around with another fellow, so I went over, and I introduced myself. I told them, "I'm Marty Kramer, production manager for Perryscope. You may not remember me," and then I refreshed his memory about Minneapolis and earlier. "I'm the kid who had Passover dessert with you and your cousin." Then I said, "Have a good show," and left them to continue talking to one another.

I moved away, but I was standing within earshot and heard Dylan say, "Where were we?" and the other fellow said, "You were telling me about Germany."

Dylan went on. "Right. It's 1983, and my manager books me on a European tour. We're in Germany. I'm a little nervous. A Jewish kid playing before a huge crowd in Germany. I get my acoustic guitar and check it. I put my harmonica on and checked it. My manager says, 'Don't worry about it, Bob. It's sold out. Nothing to worry about.' In those days, I can't remember if it was sixty or eighty thousand people, but it was massive.

One of the biggest things I've ever done outdoors. I've got butterflies. My manager says we're going to make an announcement, and then you're going to go out. 'Ladies and gentlemen, from America, Mr. Bob Dylan.' I go out to the center mic. The spotlight and festival lights come on, and I look. As far as I can see, there are people. I'm stunned for a moment. I don't know what to do. I come up to the mike and say, 'Hi. I'm one you didn't get.' Standing ovation. I had yet to play a note."

8

I Named My Little Baby Girl Holly, Buddy

A note from Marty: I was only eleven years old when the great Buddy Holly died in a tragic plane crash along with Richie Valens and J.P. "The Big Bopper" Richardson on a cold February night near Clear Lake, Iowa, so I never got to see him, let alone work with him. But his music lives on and by a strange coincidence, is inextricably tied both to my friend and co-author David and me. But I'll let David tell you the first part of the story.

David:

As a preamble, let me tell you that as an overweight, socially awkward youth, I was a major fan of Buddy Knox, someone whom I consider to be one of the founders of rock 'n' roll. I couldn't dance to save my life, but somehow when Buddy Knox's "Party Doll," "Rock My Little Baby to Sleep," "Lovey Dovey," or "Devil Woman" were played, suddenly even I could dance, not well, but passably. And between 1957 and 1961, there was one great song after another, "I Think I'm Going to Kill Myself," "Hula Love," "Storm Clouds," "Somebody Touched Me," and a dozen more. Then, suddenly in 1962, Buddy disappeared from the scene. There was, of course, no internet, so I just assumed he had fallen prey to one of the many temptations that afflicted rock artists: booze, drugs, whatever. I moved on with folk music, women, and my legal career, in no particular order. But Buddy's music stayed close to my heart.

Fast forward to a winter day in the early eighties. I was sitting in my office in the middle of Nowhere, North America, when my receptionist called me on the intercom and said, "There's a gentleman here who'd like to see you. He doesn't have an appointment. His name is Buddy Knox."

I laughed and said, "Send him in."

A moment later, a nice-looking fellow in cowboy boots and a cowboy hat walked into my office and thanked me for seeing him. I told him it was a pleasure, asked him to sit down, and asked how I could help him.

With a rich Southern accent, he said, "I understand you're the best entertainment lawyer in these here parts."

I laughed and replied, "I believe I'm the only entertainment lawyer in these here parts, so I guess by process of elimination, I may very well be the best. What can I do for you?"

He said, "Well, I'm a singer and I'd like you to represent me."

I said, "I've got to be honest. If your real name is Humbert Shimmelfennick and you can't sing to save your life, you've chosen a name that happens to be one of my favorite artists of all time, so I'll be happy to represent you."

He said, "No, that's my real name, Buddy Knox."

I said, "Sure it is, and you just happen to be here in the middle of nowhere."

And then over coffee, and later over time, he told me the rest of the story.

Buddy was born in the tiny Texas panhandle town of Happy in 1933. On the recommendation of his friend Roy Orbison from Wink, Texas, Buddy traveled to Norman Petty's homemade recording studio in Clovis, New Mexico. The session yielded "Party Doll," which was eventually scooped up by Roulette Records, which ostensibly was owned by Morris "Mo" Levy, but unknown to Buddy reputedly Levy was fronting for the New York-based Genovese crime family.

"Party Doll" became an instant number-one hit around the world, and as Buddy put it, "One minute I was on a farm in Happy, Texas, and the next on The Ed Sullivan Show. I'd never seen buildings over three stories before." Following a stint in the army reserve, Buddy followed this up with "Rock Your Little Baby to Sleep" and one hit after another. He was the first rockabilly artist to write his own number-one hit. By the end of 1957, Buddy had four million-selling singles, but little to show for it.

He told me that he went in to see Mo Levy one day to inquire as to when he would be receiving some money. Levy laughed and said, "We gave you a convertible. What else do you want?" Buddy said, "I'd like to be paid for my songs and my records." According to Buddy, Levy said,

"Your records? Your songs? They're not yours. We own them and we own you. Now get the fuck out of here." Then he picked up his phone, said something, and two thugs came in and took Buddy by the arm and led him out of the office.

"Both Bobby Darin and Connie Francis warned me about Morris Levy, and I should have listened," he later said. Roulette ended up with everything, and he got nothing.

Levy was later found guilty of extortion but died before serving any jail time.

It wasn't in Buddy's nature to make war or to stay in ostensible servitude, so in 1961 he left the organized music business and struck out on his own, making records and performing in small gigs. He never again had a charted song. In 1974, while performing at a gig, Buddy met Mitzy Shelby. A relationship bloomed, and they ultimately married and settled in the small farm town of Dominion City, some 40 miles outside of my city.

Shortly after the release of "Party Doll" in 1957, Buddy Holly came to visit Buddy at his home in Happy, and the two became good friends. After Buddy Holly died in 1959, Buddy Knox released a tribute song to his friend, a lilting ballad written by Lee Jackson called "I Named My Little Girl Holly."

So I named my little baby girl Holly, Buddy
Ever since you left this world, golly, Buddy
It's been said time and again
Soon the memory will end
But that will be the day my friend
Buddy Holly.

The eighties weren't kind to Buddy. He smoked and drank too much and sometimes lamented over how he'd been screwed over by Levy. His health suffered, and there were marital problems. The last time I saw Buddy was when I had my partner look after his divorce for him, since I didn't do that kind of work. Shortly thereafter, Buddy left for Vancouver, British Columbia. But I never forgot the ten years I'd been privileged to have Buddy Knox as my client and, more importantly, as my friend.

Over the course of our relationship, Buddy often talked about the gods of rock and roll like Buddy Holly, Roy Orbison, and Elvis, but never in a pretentious way. He was always unassuming and talked about them in the same way any of us might talk about our old friends. He had played with Holly and Orbison over the years and was friends with Elvis and visited him on occasion over the years but never played with him. What was even more endearing about Buddy was his lack of bitterness over the cards that life had dealt him. Immediately after the release of "Party Doll" and its rise to the top of the charts, Buddy was called into service by the army and missed the opportunity to cash in on his success with touring, as other artists had done. Unlike Buddy Holly, Buddy was never business-oriented, and accordingly, Levy and Roulette managed to strip Buddy of all his songs and royalties. But Buddy just took it in stride. When Buddy died, he was most certainly one of the wealthiest men I've ever known. He was devoid of any material assets whatsoever, but he had literally hundreds of thousands of people around the world who loved him and his music.

Buddy was proud and yet humble, incredibly talented yet self-effacing, gracious, and generous to a fault, and handled bounty and penuriousness with the same grace and equanimity. He was the first to offer to help someone out and was known as one of the truly nice guys of rock and roll. Always the quiet Southerner with the infectious Southern accent. He loved his family, people in general, and his music. He was quite simply a gentle man and a gentleman.

When we started working on Marty's book, I happened to ask him if he'd ever had the occasion to do any work for Buddy Knox. I'll let him pick up the story from there.

Marty:

It was the early nineties, and Les Vogt, the owner of the *Legends of Rock and Roll,* gave me a call. Buddy Knox had moved to Vancouver but had fallen on difficult times. Les had a ranch near Kelowna and encouraged Buddy to come to live there, which Buddy did until he passed away. He also arranged bookings for Buddy when Buddy was able to go out and do them, and whenever there was a booking, I would be the road manager and look after things for him. Buddy suffered a fall in February 1999 and damaged his hip. When he went to see the doctor, he was diagnosed with bone cancer and passed away less than two weeks later.

David knew Buddy for many years more than I did, but for the years I got to know Buddy and consider him a friend, I always found him to be what we call in Yiddish, a *feine mensch*, a fine man of honor and integrity. Cheerful, generous, caring, humble, enjoying every day as if it were his last, and treating everybody as if they mattered. It's kind of hard to describe, but when you get to spend time with someone like Buddy Knox who changed the whole direction of music and whose music made such a major impact on the industry, and yet he never considered himself as special and always seemed more concerned with others than with himself, it's hard not to feel like you're in the company of greatness.

Like many of the truly greats, Buddy passed away much too early. His son, Michael Knox, picked up the mantle and is a renowned music producer in Nashville, a winner of multiple Academy of Country Music awards, has produced 23 number-one hits, and is acknowledged to be a leader in the industry. I imagine when he's not up there singing Rockabilly with Buddy Holly and Roy Orbison, Buddy is looking down with incredible pride.

I never had any children, but if I had, I would have named my little boy or girl Knox, Buddy.

9

ROLL OVER BEETHOVEN, CHUCK BERRY JUST JOINED THE CHOIR

The great Chuck Berry died on March 18, 2017, at the age of 90, leaving behind a legacy matched only by Elvis, the Beatles, and the Stones.

Put aside for the moment that he was nicknamed "The Father of Rock and Roll." Forget about the fact that many of the great performers through the ages have attempted to imitate his showmanship, with his one-legged hop and his "duck walk" routine, none ever as good as the master. Don't mention that he refined and developed rhythm and blues into what became the most distinctive elements of rock 'n' roll or that *Rolling Stone* named him fifth on the list of the one hundred greatest artists of all time. Consider just his musical legacy, his songs:

Elvis Presley covered "Too Much Monkey Business"
Jimi Hendrix covered "Johnny B. Goode"
The Beatles covered "Rock and Roll Music," "Roll Over Beethoven," and "Memphis, Tennessee"
The Rolling Stones covered "Come On" and "Let It Rock"
The Beach Boys copied "Sweet Little Sixteen" in "Surfin U.S.A"

Carl Perkins covered "Roll Over Beethoven" and "Johnny B. Goode"
AC/DC covered "School Days"
David Bowie slightly altered "Around and Around"
The Yardbirds covered "Guitar Boogie" as "Jeff's Boogie"
The Kinks covered "Too Much Monkey Business" and
Buddy Holly covered "Brown Eyed Handsome Man"

Just a small scratch on the surface of the artists who have covered his incredible music catalog.

John Lennon said, "If you tried to give rock and roll another name, you might call it Chuck Berry." Ted Nugent said, "If you don't know every Chuck Berry lick, you can't play rock guitar." Bob Dylan called Chuck Berry "the Shakespeare of rock and roll." Bruce Springsteen tweeted, "Chuck Berry was rock's greatest practitioner, guitarist, and the greatest pure rock 'n' roll writer who ever lived. Perhaps Leonard Cohen summed it up best when he reportedly said, "All of us are footnotes to the words of Chuck Berry."

I had the great honor of meeting with and working for Chuck Berry and have no story to tell about him, other than he was a gentleman and gracious to work with, and watching him perform was an experience you never forget. Like listening to Jascha Heifetz play a Stradivarius or watching Sir Laurence Olivier play Othello. You just knew you were in the presence of greatness. I do, however, have a story to tell about his road manager.

On the day of the performance, I was waiting for Chuck and his road manager when they arrived at the theater. I got Chuck settled in his dressing room and then proceeded to assist his road manager in the various functions he needed to attend to prior to showtime. When all of this was completed, his road manager told me that the dressing room, food, catering, lights, and sound were all great. Everything was satisfactory. Then he asked me about Chuck's guitar. I wasn't quite sure what he was talking about and asked for clarification. He indicated that Chuck's rider required that we have a special gold Gibson guitar available for Chuck's use. It was a relatively rare type of guitar not used by a lot of performers. I brought out my notes, and he was correct that it had been a specific requirement in the rider. I explained that this wasn't something I looked after, but I would check with my sound and lights technical guy, whom I was confident would have arranged for it to be there.

I found my tech guy, who confirmed that he had in fact obtained the required guitar and fetched it for me. He told me he had obtained it from a local collector who was highly knowledgeable in these matters. I took the case and was returning to Chuck's dressing room when I ran into his road manager. I told him I had found the guitar and gave it to him. He said, "Let me take a look." He opened the case, took one look at the guitar, and said, "It's the wrong one." I replied that the chap we had obtained it from confirmed it was absolutely the exact guitar Chuck generally used, but the road manager was adamant and said, "Get me the right one or we won't have a show."

I knew that in situations such as this, arguing would get me nowhere, and we still had a couple of hours until showtime, so I said, "I'm not a guitar guy. Leave it with me. I'll get it straightened out.

I went back to my tech guy, who said his guy was reliable and this was the right guitar. I said, "Let me call him."

I called the fellow, told him who I was, and that Chuck's road manager said it was the wrong guitar. He asked me if I was a guitarist and when I said I'm not, he said he didn't want to talk to me, and if we didn't want the guitar, he'd come right down and pick it up and I could go screw myself. I told him I've got the guitar and it's beautiful, but the road manager said it's not the right one. He told me to get him on the phone and he'd give him a piece of his mind. I said, "Let me ask you something. How common are these?" He said, "They're not. I've got the only one in town. Marty, there's none other than mine. Trust me. I don't know you, but this is the one." I told him that my tech spoke highly of him, and he should leave it with me, and thanked him.

I grabbed the case and was heading back towards Chuck's dressing room when I ran into the road manager in the hall. I said, "You were right. I'm going to exchange it now. I'll be right back." He asked how long, and I told him half an hour.

I went down the back stairs to the parking lot, put the guitar case in my truck, and locked the door. Then I crossed the street and walked to the corner for a couple of slices of pizza and a drink. A half hour later, I went back to my truck, grabbed the guitar case, and proceeded back into the theater. I went to the stage and got the tech to take the guitar out of the case and place it on the guitar stand in the middle of the stage, displayed like a fine work of art. Meanwhile, I went and fetched the road manager and brought him to the stage. He took one look and said, "There you go. That's it. That's the right one. Sorry to be tough with you, but we're hardball players. Welcome to the team."

Hey, the road manager may have been a bit of a putz, but Chuck Berry was The Man, and I was happy to be a team player for him any day of the week.

10

THEM'S THE BREAKS

Years ago, we used to do the Sturgis, South Dakota motorcycle rally. For ten days in the first full week of August, around half a million or more bikers descend on the small town of Sturgis for a big gathering. Over the years, BTO were the headliners, since several of their songs like "Roll on Down the Highway" and "Let It Ride" were anthems for the bikers. On one occasion, Gerry Meyers, who used to manage several bands and was a close friend of mine, was down there on his motorcycle. It was the early days of cell phones, and I had one of those big 2-pound phones. Gerry called me and said, "I'm in Sturgis. I'll be down by the main stage near the infield. Call me when you get here."

Once we got down there, I made contact again and told him we were in town. I told Gerry where we were, and he said, "I'm at a tent near you. Come on over. There's somebody I want you to meet," and gave us directions. I had no idea who it was, but Randy and I wandered over.

I thought he was in one of the catering tents, but he was in a tent in one of the designated areas. We entered the tent and weren't in there for more than a few moments when Gerry came over with another man and said, "I want you to meet Sonny Barger. This is Randy Bachman and my old friend Marty Kramer." Sonny said, "Pleased to meet you. By the way, welcome to Sturgis."

Now, for those of you not familiar with the name, Sonny Barger was one of the founding members of the Hell's Angels, and because of several books he'd written and films he'd appeared in, he was considered by many to be the head of the Angels.

Sonny looked at Randy and then said, "Tonight, when you perform, one of our personal favorites is 'Born to Be Wild.'" Randy immediately replied, "You've got me mistaken with Steppenwolf. We don't perform 'Born to Be Wild.'" Sonny shot back, "I'd like you to perform that for us tonight. You're here." Randy said, "We've got to go. We've got things to do. But I don't think we'll be performing that song because we don't do that." Sonny then extended his hand to me and said, "It's been very nice meeting you," and shook my hand. Then Randy extended his own hand to shake Sonny's, and Sonny interlocked his fingers with Randy's, then said, "And remember you'll be doing 'Born to Be Wild' tonight." Randy just went *Oooh owww,* and by the time we were out of the tent, we realized his little finger was dislocated and bent out of shape. We went to the nurse's tent, got his finger fixed up, and taped it to the next finger. That night in the middle of the performance, Randy announced, "We've been here many times, and we'd like to dedicate this next song to the boys in the tent over there." pointing to the Hell's Angels tent and he played "Born to Be Wild" which was never ever in the BTO set before.

When you wish somebody good luck in show business, you generally say "Break a leg." I suppose it's possible Sonny may have misunderstood the concept and thought it was "Break a finger."

11

SERIOUS MUSIC, SERIOUS BUSINESS

Considered by many as one of the twentieth century's most influential musicians, with album sales of more than one hundred and forty million, David Bowie may have been one of the most interesting and iconic musicians with whom I ever had the pleasure of working. I was involved with part of his *Serious Moonlight Tour* and worked with him on a day-to-day basis. He was always very cordial, a nice man, but unlike most of the artists I've worked with, it wasn't a Marty-David relationship. He was generally involved in all the details of the tour and maintained a somewhat formal demeanor. But always friendly.

Like me, Bowie was a collector, but just in the world of art. After his death, his family decided to sell part of his collection owing to a lack of space to store it. Accordingly, three auctions were held at Sotheby's in London, representing about 65% of Bowie's collection. The auctions attracted over 50,000 visitors, and the auction itself was attended by 1750 bidders, with over 1,000 bidding online. The overall sales totaled more than $40 million. Not too shabby for a kid from a family of modest means from Brixton, South London, whose junior school choir director only considered his voice "adequate."

12

FOREVER YOUNG

There are many stories I could share with you about the great Neil Young, having known him since we were both teenagers and with whom I worked on numerous occasions. But I am only going to tell you one point of interest and one story, which I believe sums up the essence of the man.

Point of interest. Neil and I are both collectors. For reasons I really can't explain, both Neil and I collect hearses. He has one which he brought with him from Winnipeg and which he named Mortimer Hearseberg. I have three, which I named Juan Wayride, Nick Rosis, and Fine Al Ride. Neil is also an avid collector of model railway trains, and I believe has one of almost every model train ever made. He also holds numerous patents for software applications he has created for model trains. All his trains are stored in a football-sized room, operational and on tracks.

Randy Bachman and I were at Neil's 3000-acre ranch on the side of a mountain outside of San Francisco, completing an album at one of Neil's two studios on the property. Neil was playing grunge on the album. During the day, we took a break and went over to the building where Neil had his office and stored his massive collection of trains. We were mid-tour, having a great time watching Neil direct hundreds of trains from a tower above the floor, when Neil's manager, Elliott Roberts, found us and spoke. "I'm sorry to interrupt, guys, but Peter Gabriel's on the phone, Neil, and he wants to talk to you about booking the studio." We're talking Peter Gabriel of Genesis fame, 6 Grammys, was voted Best Male Vocal, 100 million records sold, was named by *Time Magazine* as one of the 100 most influential men in the world, and was awarded a Man of Peace Award by the Nobel Committee.

Neil said, "Do me a favor, Elliott. Tell Peter I'm with friends, playing with my trains. I'll call him later." Now there's a lesson in priorities and friendship.

13

Pretty Woman, Beautiful Man

I imagine it's become clear by now that whatever success I've managed to achieve in the music industry is due in no small part to the kindness of my friends and the confidence they've shown in me. A perfect example is my history with the legendary Roy Orbison. I'm somewhat conflicted, being undecided as to where I should start, but I think my friend Les Vogt, who has always been committed to his artists would insist I start with the artist, so I shall do that.

With a career that lasted only 25 years, fraught with tragedy, Roy Orbison achieved what most artists couldn't have imagined accomplishing in double or triple that time. More than 75 albums, 75 charted singles, 7 Grammy's, inducted into the Songwriters Hall of Fame, the Rock and Roll Hall of Fame, Pop Music Hall of Fame, and the Memphis Music Hall of Fame, named by *Rolling Stone* as number 37 on the list of the Greatest Artists of All time and number 13 on the list of the Greatest Singers of All Time. Composer of such iconic songs as "Only the Lonely," "Running Scared," "Claudette," "Blue Bayou," "Crying," "In Dreams," and "Pretty Woman," and co-founder of the pop supergroup The Travelling Wilburys with George Harrison, Bob Dylan, Tom Petty, and Jeff Lynne, all before his premature death of a heart attack at age 52.

What makes these accomplishments even more amazing is that in the middle of his career, he was devastated by two unbearable tragedies, the death of his beloved wife Claudette in a motorcycle accident in 1966, and then two years later, the death of two of his sons in a house fire in Tennessee when he was away on a concert tour. But more on Roy in a moment.

First, let me tell you a little bit about my friend Les Vogt. In the early 1960s, Les, a former rock singer, formed a concert production company with his friend Red Robinson. One of their first projects was a trio of Roy Orbison concerts. One of their venues was in a city with strict rules about rock and roll shows on the Sabbath, so Les decided to circumvent this rule by starting the concert at midnight on Sunday. Orbison was concerned that nobody would attend a concert that late at night, but his concerns were unfounded, and fans lined up around the block. It was a huge financial success, and although there was no obligation on his part, Les paid Orbison a large bonus.

More than a decade later, when Orbison's career was on a decline, Les was surprised to find Orbison playing small venues and offered him a Canadian tour, which proved to be so successful that Roy invited Les to move to Nashville to become his U.S. manager. While managing Roy, Les booked him into a concert in Santa Monica, which was attended by many superstars and ultimately led to the formation of The Travelling Wilburys. While Les was managing Roy, he hired me as Roy's road manager.

What you probably didn't know about Roy Orbison was that he was an extremely quiet, self-effacing man. He rarely said more than a few words during his concerts and was generally quiet and reserved both before and after. He was always remarkably polite, considerate, and accommodating. In *The Immortals – The Great Artists of All Time*, k.d. lang compared Roy to a tree, with passive but solid beauty, and that probably summed it up. He performed standing still, dressed in black with dark sunglasses. Roy himself once said, "I'm not a super-personality, on stage or off. People come to hear my music, my songs. That is what I give them."

Talking with Roy was like listening to a history of rock 'n' roll since he played with and knew most of the greats. Roy would talk about his early days in Texas, being referred to Sam Phillips by Johnny Cash, meeting with the Everly Brothers and their recording his song "Claudette," and traveling with the Beatles and The Rolling Stones. I remember Roy talking about composing songs and how it could take months to write a bad song, but generally, the good ones came from inspiration of one kind or another, and he could write them in twenty minutes. In 1961, he wrote "Crying" shortly after running into a girlfriend with whom he'd recently broken up, and after some small talk and then leaving, he felt tears running down his cheeks. He was concerned about writing a song about it since a man admitting he cried wasn't the thing to do, but he didn't care. He went home and wrote:

I was all right for a while
I could smile for awhile
But I saw you last night
You held my hand so tight
As you stopped to say hello.
Oh, you wished me well
You, you couldn't tell
That I'd been
Crying over you
Crying over you

As an aside, he mentioned how on his 1965 Australian tour with the Rolling Stones, they became good friends. He played "Pretty Woman" for them, and they loved the backbeat from the song after he sang the words "Pretty Woman," and that evolved into "I Can't Get No Satisfaction."

People often wondered about Roy's sunglasses and if he had problems with his eyes. Roy told me the story behind the sunglasses. He was traveling on a private jet on the way to a concert and forgot his regular glasses on the plane. He wore only his sunglasses on stage that night. He then left on a commercial flight to begin his tour with the Beatles in Europe and still only had the sunglasses, so he wore them there as well. For whatever reason, by the end of the tour, they had become part of his legend, so he continued to wear them on stage for the rest of his career as part of his on-stage wardrobe. Occam's razor. The explanation that requires the least speculation is usually the correct one.

Roy was a man of few words. I remember in one of the last interviews he gave before his death, he was asked after all that he had accomplished, how he would like to be remembered, and Roy responded, "I'd just like to be remembered." He needn't have been concerned.

14

THE WIZARD OF OZZIE AND HARRIET

Just as in the non-entertainment world, good people die, often much too soon. When we think of artists who left the scene too early, the names that most often come to mind are people like Elvis, Jim Morrison, Jimi Hendrix, Janis Joplin, Duane Allman, Buddy Holly, Ritchie Valens, Jim Croce, Kurt Cobain, Brian Jones, Hank Williams, Tim Buckley, and Amy Winehouse just to scratch the surface. One name that is often forgotten is one of the true music greats, actor, musician, and singer-songwriter Ricky Nelson.

From age eight, Ricky starred on the radio and then on television in the series *The Adventures of Ozzie and Harriet* with his parents and his brother David. In 1957, he embarked on a recording career and subsequently placed 53 songs on the *Billboard* Hot 100, his first being "Poor Little Fool." He recorded 19 additional Top 10 hits. His Stone Canyon Band featured Randy Meisner, who became a founding member of The Eagles. From 1957 to 1962, Ricky had 30 Top-40 hits, more than any other artist except Elvis Presley and Pat Boone. In addition, Nelson had a highly successful film career.

I met Ricky for the first time when he was at the height of his recording and touring career. It was after he had recorded "Hello, Mary Lou" that we got to chatting, and he asked me if I knew who had written it. I, of course, did and told him it was Gene Pitney. That solidified the relationship. I didn't see him until later when I looked after him on a comeback tour, but he was the same unassuming, friendly man he had been when we first met, and a pleasure to work with and be around.

When you've been in the business for as long as I've been, it's not unusual to find yourself working with second generations of artists. Some of these that I've had the privilege of working with are Ringo Starr's son Zak, Jackie Wilson's son Bobby Brooks Wilson, and Randy Bachman's son Tal. All of these are extremely talented and fine young men, and a credit to their parents. Regrettably, I didn't have the opportunity to meet Rick's sons Matthew and Gunnar until after Rick had passed away. Their band, Nelson, achieved success during the early 90s, and their album *After the Rain* went double-platinum and featured the number-one hit singles "Can't Live Without Your Love" and "Affection." Randy Bachman and I were at Midem, the international annual music conference in Cannes, France, and ran into Gunner and Matthew. It turned out to be a mutual admiration society, and Randy and the boys agreed to perform together, which they did on "Takin' Care of Business."

Now, just in case you're ever a contestant on *Jeopardy*, and the question is "They are the only family to achieve number-one record status in three successive generations," the answer is "Who are the Nelsons?" Rick's parents, Ozzie and Harriet, first, then Ricky, and finally Matthew and Gunner.

15

YOU WERE ALWAYS ON MY MIND

When I first sat down to write this book, I made myself a promise that I wouldn't dwell on my artists' substance abuse for several reasons. First and most importantly, I have always stuck to the rule that "What happens in Vegas stays in Vegas." My artists trusted that what they did in front of me would be kept confidential, and I have tried to live up to that trust. Also, from a practical point of view, since the world of music is perhaps intertwined with drug use more than any other profession other than the Sinaloa Cartel, if I were to talk about artists and drugs, I would probably have to add another 400 pages.

I believe I have adhered to that rule throughout the book, but I am going to make one exception, and that is for the beloved icon known by everyone merely as Willie. Singer, songwriter, musician, actor, producer, author, poet, and activist, Willie has been a mainstay on the American scene for more than 65 years, and I believe for most of that time he has been half-baked, and this was certainly true when I knew him. I am telling you this only because Willie told everyone. In fact, in a recent article in *Rolling Stone* magazine, Willie credited cannabis with saving his life. As an alternative to alcohol and drugs throughout his life, Willie said, "I think weed kept me from wanting to kill people. And probably kept a lot of people from wanting to kill me, too – out there drunk, running around."

But here's the thing. Even half-baked, Willie never gave a performance that was less than outstanding.

His legacy is almost unbelievable:

- More than 70 solo studio albums
- 47 film appearances
- 9 books
- 13 Grammys
- 7 American Music Awards
- 10 CMA Awards
- 5 Academy of Country Music Awards
- Library of Congress Gershwin Award
- President of the Board of Farm Aid
- 33 #1 singles, including his compositions "On the Road Again" and "Angel Flying Too Close to the Ground"
- Hundreds of songs written

Despite accomplishing all of that, Willie never changed. I remember doing a tour with Willie and Waylon Jennings. Once we arrived at that day's location, I would look after the setup and sound checks. Willie would always be there, but Waylon generally stayed on his tour bus, and Willie's drummer, who looked a lot like Waylon, would fill in for him. Of course, we all knew about this, but Waylon's fans who gathered round to watch not only assumed it was Waylon, but they would also shout approvingly how he never sounded better. After we had completed all our setup, Willie would go and mingle with his fans, just to say hello and thank them for coming. It would never have occurred to him to do any different. And I don't believe he's ever changed over all these years. He never looked at himself as anything but one of the people. Just Willie.

Over the years I've had the pleasure of working with most of the greatest country artists, including Vince Gill, Glen Campbell, Loretta Lynn, Hank Williams Jr., Waylon Jennings, Carl Perkins, The Oak Ridge Boys, George Fox, Michelle Wright, The Bellamy Brothers, Travis Tritt, Ricky Van Shelton, The Gatlin Brothers, The Georgia Satellites, Tanya Tucker, Dwight Yokum and Tammy Wynette, to name just some of them. But if I had to name the greatest of them all, it would be no contest. Just Willie.

I have only two other comments to make about Willie.

Firstly, in response to criticism about General Ulysses S. Grant's imbibing, Abraham Lincoln said, "If I could find out what brand of whiskey Grant drank, I would send a barrel of it to all the other commanders." I think a lot of performers might consider smoking whatever Willie smokes; and secondly, although I take no issue with Willie and Waylon's great song, "Mammas Don't Let Your Babies Grow Up to be Cowboys," I think we should all be forever grateful to Nancy Nelson, Willie's grandmother who raised him, that she never adhered to this advice when raising young Willie.

16

ROLLING DOWN THE RIVER

We recently lost another legend. The great Tina Turner passed away at her home in Switzerland, where she'd been living for decades, as Europe was always more accepting of her both as a person and as an artist than her homeland, and where she found happiness with her husband, hugely successful record producer and promoter Erwin Bach. He gave her one of his kidneys a few years ago to help battle one of her many life challenging illnesses.. Although acknowledged as a superstar in America, in Europe, she was bigger than the Rolling Stones. Twelve Grammy awards (8 competitive and four honorary), more than 150 million records sold worldwide, sold-out concerts of up to more than 180,000 (the largest paying audience for a solo performer), first woman on the cover of *Rolling Stone*, Kennedy Center Honours recipient, and beloved by the likes of Mick Jagger, Oprah, Cher, Eric Clapton, and Beyoncé.

I first met Tina and had the privilege of working with her in the mid-80s when I was contacted by her management to put a band together for her in Vancouver. The drummer in that band was Garry Peterson of The Guess Who. Many years later, I worked with her when she was on tour performing in large Stadiums.

To understand a major star best, you must see how they treat the most important and least important people in their retinue, although that's usually not the same. In my experience, truly great artists like Ringo Starr treat everyone the same, with kindness and respect. And that's exactly how Tina treated everybody. And watching her perform was like watching the few exceptions in the entertainment world. She owned the stage. Every move, every note, everything she did was perfect.

She was most definitely the Queen of Rock and Roll.

The legitimate Queen has passed. You'll be greatly missed, Proud Mary. You're simply the best. Better than all the rest.

17

QUITE SIMPLY THE GREATEST

Coming of age in the fifties and sixties, it was natural that my musical tastes gravitated towards rock 'n' roll. But unless you grew up in a cave somewhere, it would have been impossible not to be aware of the three artists who, more than any others occupied every aspect of the music world, movies, TV, comedy, and live entertainment. I am, of course talking about Frank Sinatra, Dean Martin, and Sammy Davis Jr. Like almost every other sentient human being of the time, to me, these three were gods. For any of my younger readers who may not be familiar with the breadth of these men's careers, I feel I must provide a summary so that you may fully appreciate why I held them in such awe.

Frank Sinatra was considered by many critics to be the greatest singer of the 20th century, as much for how he would interpret a song as for his voice. He sold over 150 million records, 60 plus albums, and won 11 Grammys. He starred in more than 50 films and won an Academy Award. He appeared as a guest on almost every major television show, was perhaps Las Vegas's major attraction for decades, and was named by *Time* magazine as one of the 20th century's most influential people.

Dean Martin recorded more than 100 albums and 600 singles. His single "Everybody Loves Somebody" knocked the Beatles' "It's a Hard Day's Night" out of the number one position in the U.S. in 1964, and Elvis was one of his biggest fans. He was awarded a Lifetime Achievement Grammy Award. He was a headliner in Las Vegas for almost three decades. He starred in more than 60 films, starting with a series of comedies with Jerry Lewis, which became the highest-grossing films of their kind, and appeared on scores of television shows, including 318 episodes of two of his own series, and won a Golden Globe.

Like Sinatra and Martin. Sammy Davis Jr. was also a triple threat. He recorded more than 35 albums with 31 charted singles, including the number one record, "Candy Man." He was also friends with Elvis. He appeared in more than 30 films and on a slew of television shows as a guest, plus hosted two of his own series and won an Emmy and a Golden Globe. He appeared in three Broadway shows and won a Tony. He was also a magnificent dancer and a masterful impersonator.

You must understand the breadth of their talent. These three men were international superstars in every iteration of the entertainment world: recording, live entertainment, television, stage, movies, comedy, musicals, and drama. There was nothing they couldn't do, individually or collectively. Except for Al Jolson a hundred years ago, I'm not aware of any entertainer who has ever approached the scope of their all-encompassing talents and dominance of the various forms of media. Elvis was a recording superstar and made a slew of films, but aside from a few specials, he never managed to penetrate television. And his career barely lasted twenty years. The Beatles were recording superstars, but other than five films and occasional television appearances, their visual recorded presence was limited. Plus, their career as a group lasted only ten years. Lady Gaga is a superstar in both recording and live performance and was brilliant in her film appearance in *A Star is Born*. But as I said, there is nobody in the past 75 years who even approaches Sinatra, Martin, and Davis with combined record sales of more than 300 million albums, combined movies of more than 140 films, and more than 500 combined television appearances, including several of their own series. Plus Sinatra's career extended over 50 years, Martin's over 52 years, and Davis's over an incredible 62 years. These men were in a galaxy of their own, and it is unlikely their kind will be seen again.

In the '60s, Sinatra, Martin, and Sammy Davis Jr. would pal around together in Las Vegas when they were performing and, together with a few of their friends, became known as The Rat Pack. Now, fast forward twenty-five years. In my wildest imagination, I never would have thought I would ever have a chance to work with even one of these legends. Then in 1988, the three of them decided to embark on their *Together Again* tour, with 28 scheduled performances. Unfortunately, Dean Martin took ill after the sixth performance and was replaced by Liza Minelli, but as fate would have it, I was retained as production manager for one of the six shows when they did perform together. The show was taking place at the Coliseum, which also served as the arena for the local NHL hockey team. The show was in the middle of March, so the ice was covered with plywood for the seating, but it still meant that some of the dressing rooms could be cold.

When they arrived, I greeted them as I always did. I introduced myself and then showed each of them to their dressing rooms. The dressing rooms were nicely furnished with a couch, a small TV, and the usual amenities. They were each accompanied by security personnel as well as a head of security who oversaw everything for them. I told them if there was anything they needed, they should let me know. Frank and Dean were fine, but Sammy found his dressing room cold and asked if I could make it warmer. There were no controls in the rooms as it had to be handled by the electricians in the building, so I told him I would take care of it, which I did.

A short time later, Frank's head of security came to me and said that Frank liked to watch the news on CNN but was unable to get that channel on the set in his dressing room, and was there anything I could do about that? I explained that there was no cable in the Coliseum, which meant that the rabbit ears on TVs only picked up local stations, but he should leave it with me, and I'd see what I could do.

I knew there was only one TV set in the building that received all outside channels, and that was in the VIP Lounge since it was serviced by a satellite on the building's roof. I headed in that direction but had to pass first through the loading docks, and on the way, encountered a cable company service man. I asked what he was doing there, and he produced a work order indicating he was supposed to do a cable connection between the VIP Lounge and the Sportscasters Box. He explained that they wanted to be able to set the satellite to feed from the TV in the Lounge to a monitor in the Press Box so that when broadcasting a game, they could receive a live feed on scores in other games to pass on to their audience. I told him I would take him to the Lounge, which I did. I asked the fellow in charge of the Lounge who was a friend, if it would be possible to take over the Lounge for a while so Frank could watch CNN, but he told me it wasn't possible as they had another function scheduled.

I gave it some thought and wandered over to the Press Box, and as I thought, saw that it was situated in almost the same position as the dressing rooms, just at a higher level. I asked the technician if, once he completed the connection from the Lounge to the Press box and we then switched on CNN in the lounge, would CNN appear on the monitor in the Sports Box. He said it would. I then asked if we ran a cable from the Press Box to the dressing room, would the TV in the dressing room receive CNN, and he said it would and could be done, depending on where the dressing room was located. I explained where it was and why I wanted to do it. He said his wife was a huge fan of Sinatra's but that they had been unable to get tickets. I, of course, told him that I controlled the guest passes as well as backstage passes, and one good turn deserved another.

And so it came to pass, although not easily. It took several hundred feet of cable, which had to be run through the ceiling of the press box and then attached to the outside wall of the Coliseum so as not to create any kind of obstacle that people might trip on, but it got done. I had to ask Frank if we could rearrange the couch and the TV, and he said, "Whatever you have to do, it's fine." Frank got his CNN and the technician, and his wife got their tickets and backstage passes.

The moment I learned I was going to be the production manager for their show, I began delving through my record collection including the extensive collection of their albums I had accumulated over the years, looking for what would be the best ones I could have them sign, if they were of a mind to do so. After we had completed all the sound checks, I went to the head of security and asked if it would be okay if I asked the guys to sign some things for me. He was very obliging and said, "By all means." I noticed he had some great color photographs for the press and asked if I could have one of them, and again, he said, "Absolutely."

I went to Frank's dressing room and knocked. He opened the door and invited me in. I asked if there was anything he needed and he said no, everything was great. Then he said, "How did you arrange for the cable feed?" I said, "You said you wanted it, so I got it." He said, "But how did you get them to run a cable up the side of the building?" I said, "Are you kidding? The cable guy was a big fan. For two tickets to the show and backstage passes, so he could meet you, I could have gotten him to attach an antenna to his ass, hang out your window and get a live feed." Frank laughed and said, "Kid, you are my kind of production manager. I like you." I said, "I've got to be honest Frank. I'm also a huge fan. I have every one of your albums. I brought one of my favorites here when I heard you were going to be performing. Would you be kind enough to sign it for me?" He said, "Of course." and signed a message on the white band of the hat he was wearing on the album cover.

I decided to push my luck and pulled the color photo from my bag and asked if he wouldn't mind signing that as well. He looked at it and said, "That's a great picture of me. Where did you get it?" I replied that it was the photo that was being given to the press. He laughed and said, "I really look good in that picture. I think I'll get it enlarged and paste it on my mirror so that's what I'll see first thing in the morning after a late night, rather than this." and pointed at his face. And then he signed it. I thanked him and told him if there was anything else, he needed to let me know and I moved on to Dean's dressing room.

I knocked on the door and Dean opened it and invited me in. I asked if there was anything he needed, and he told me that everything was fine. Then as with Frank, I explained how I was a big fan and produced an album of his greatest hits and asked if he would mind signing it for me. Dean looked at the record and said, "I honestly don't remember ever recording this. I must have been looped at the time." I said, "Really?" He laughed and said, "I'm just kidding. The hard-drinking is just part of the act. Most of the time I don't drink any more than the next guy. Assuming the next guy is Frank." And then he broke up laughing. Then he signed it and signed the color photo as well.

I should mention that the rider to their contract only provided for things like coffee, tea, and water, so it's quite likely that what Dean mentioned about the drinking all being part of the act was probably true. But it was an integral part. When it came time for the performance, Dean opened the show, clowning around with booze gags. Sipping from a cocktail glass, looking slightly tipsy, he would ask the audience in a slurred voice, "How long have I been on?' It brought down the house.

Finally, I moved on to Sammy's dressing room and repeated the process. He invited me in, and I inquired if the heat was satisfactory, and he told me it was perfect. Then I produced two sets of rare extended play records of his from my carrying case and asked him if he'd mind signing a set for me as I was a huge fan. He looked at them and remarked how rare they were, that he hadn't seen them for years and didn't have copies himself. He asked if I wanted him to sign both sets and I said no, I had brought the extra set for him, as I had two sets. He said, "Really? Wow, you are a mensch." And then Sammy who had converted to Judaism in 1962, smiled and added, "You're Jewish, right?" With a straight face, I said, "Seriously Sammy? How could anybody look at either one of us and not immediately know that we were Jewish." He broke up and gave me a huge hug. He also signed the color photo.

Sammy Davis Jr. called me a mensch and hugged me. Dean Martin made jokes with me. Frank Sinatra said he liked me. How does it get better than that? I have no doubt that the three of them are entertaining everybody up there every night. I only hope that once I get there, the position of the road, no make that cloud, tour and production manager is still open.

3

WHILE THE MUSIC PLAYED

18

THE ARTISTS ALWAYS COME FIRST (BUT THEIR PETS ARE A CLOSE SECOND)

One of my favorite memories involves my one and only interaction with royalty.

It was the early 1980s and Yul Brynner had begun his last national tour of *The King and I.* In Los Angeles, only hours before his 4000th performance of the play, he received test results indicating that he had inoperable lung cancer. He was forced to take several months off for radiation therapy and then the tour resumed. I was engaged as his body man when he came to our city for an extended one-month run. He had rented a million-dollar house for two months in the affluent area of town, not far from the theatre. I imagine nowadays that house probably sells in the eight figures. It was beautiful.

When Mr. Brynner arrived, he was already full of cancer. He kept it a secret however and looking at him you would never know. He looked as strong and vital as he had in the 40 or 50 times I had watched him in *The Magnificent Seven.* Not long after he first arrived, however, a delivery truck showed up at the house and they delivered this large cancer bed, it looked like an iron lung, which was where he slept every night.

He had received some death threats before coming to the city, so every day I charted different routes to and from the theater. I also engaged two off-duty policemen who followed us everywhere in an unmarked car. During the performance, the police were stationed on either side of the stage with instructions to shoot to kill and ask questions later in the event of any incident. Fortunately, the only incident during Mr. Brynner's stay concerned Tigi.

The Brynners had a Chinese Shar-Pei that looked like Charles Laughton at age 90. The dog was six months old and basically still untrained, but a lovely puppy, nevertheless. It was my job to look after him, and because he wasn't fully housetrained, he was confined to the summer kitchen and hallway in the house the Brynners were renting. I had to lay diapers all over the floor to prevent damage. I also had to ensure that the car I drove the Brynners around in had leather seats that wouldn't be damaged in the event of a little puppy incontinence.

Every morning I would pick up a copy of the *New York Times* and bring it to the house. Mr. Brynner would read it while eating breakfast and I would walk Tigi. After that, we'd head to the theatre. When I was no longer required there, I would take Tigi and we would drive around town until we were needed. Tigi loved me, which was understandable. I changed his diapers and was his personal chauffeur after all.

As I mentioned, the only incident of consequence involved Tigi. It occurred when we had arranged a large party at the house to celebrate Mr. Brynner's birthday. Somebody opened the door to the summer kitchen and Tigi made a beeline to an incredibly expensive velvet Chesterfield, hopped on board, and then anointed it. Fortunately, I was able to grab him and clean it as best I could before the off-duty cops could shoot him.

While he was at the house, Mr. Brynner, who had started smoking at age 12, recorded an anti-smoking PSA. After the filming was completed, he told me that the next time I saw this commercial he'd be dead as he had specifically asked that it not be aired until he died from the effects of smoking.

Almost everybody who worked for Mr. Brynner called him Mr. King or King. Over the period that I was working for him, we became friends, and he would insist that I call him Yul. But I never could. He was the legendary gunfighter Chris Adams in *The Magnificent Seven*. He was the King in 4,000-plus Broadway performances and the movie *The King and I*. You don't call Queen Elizabeth "Liz" and you don't call the King "Yul." He was always Mr. Brynner to me.

One day we were talking in his dressing room and the subject of children came up. Mr. Brynner told me they had adopted two of their children, his daughters Mia and Melody. Then he told me that there was an interesting story concerning them that only a few of his closest friends knew. He explained:

"My wife Jacqueline Thion de la Chaume came from Vietnam. Years ago during the Vietnam War, she told me there were 30 or 40 orphans in the village where she grew up and she wanted to go back to that village and get those orphans out. So when the war ended, I said let's do it. I know a lot of powerful people, so I had my secretary set up a meeting with President Gerald Ford. I told him I wanted to go to Vietnam. He asked, "To perform?"

I said, "No, I want to go on a mission to get orphan children from my wife's village out of the country.

"That's still a war zone," he said. "The answer is no."

So I started wondering how could I do this. Then I get a brainstorm. I called up my old friend Hugh Hefner and I said, "Here's what I want to do. I want to go to Vietnam. I want to land a 747 there, and I want to bring back a bunch of orphans."

Hef's answer was "When do you want to go?"

I answered, "As soon as you can arrange it."

"We'll take the *Playboy* 747," Hef said. He got the pilot and a bunch of *Playboy* Bunnies to babysit the kids, and he furnished the interior of the 747 with a playroom full of all sorts of toys and candies. Then we decided we'd need some experienced military types, so he got 20 guys from SWAT teams and ex-Special Forces with full equipment. We flew to Vietnam and landed in a massive field not far from the village, a deserted former U.S. airstrip. Recognizance showed it was abandoned. There was no tower so we did an instrument landing. The military guys ran into the jungle and a while later returned with around 40 kids. We loaded them onto the plane and flew back to the States. We put all but two of them up for adoption and my wife and I adopted those two, Mia and Melody. The U.S. government didn't help. Between Hef and myself, we financed the whole thing.

He may not have had royal lineage, but he was one king who was true nobility.

19

ANYTHING YOU CAHN DO, I CAHN DO BETTER

One of the greatest moments of my life was getting to look after Sammy Cahn. For a music aficionado like me, meeting Sammy Cahn was akin to an English literature student getting to meet William Shakespeare.

Sammy was an American lyricist, songwriter, and musician. He was not just *a* lyricist; he was the best. He had four Academy Awards, 31 Academy Award nominations, five Golden Globes, and an Emmy just to name a few of his honors. More importantly, his songs are a history of American 20th-century music. They include "Three Coins in the Fountain," "All The Way," "High Hopes," "Call Me Irresponsible," "I'll Walk Alone," "I'll Never Stop Loving You," "The Best of Everything," "The Second Time Around," "My Kind of Town," "I Guess I'll Hang My Tears Out To Dry," and so many more I could go on for pages. He wrote for Broadway, movies, and television. His "Love and Marriage" was the theme song for the TV hit *Married with Children*.

Sammy was a guest star on *The Paul Anka Show*, which was taped in Vancouver. I picked him up at the airport. It was winter. He was wearing a white fur coat and white fur hat and looked like a snowman. Sammy was born on the Lower East side of New York in 1913, the son of Jewish immigrants from Galicia. He had worked in Vaudeville and in the Catskill Mountains and spoke fluent Yiddish, which I did also, so we bonded fairly quickly.

While we were driving from the airport, he said, "I want to tell you something. Do you know who I am? I'm Sammy Cahn. I'm the world's foremost lyricist."

"I know who you are," I said. "And I agree. I believe you're the greatest lyricist in the world. But to be fair, it's a lot easier to be a famous lyricist when you're from New York than if you're from Canada."

"Why is that?" he asked.

"Well," I said, "putting aside that Tin Pan Alley and Broadway are in New York, it's little things. The Canadian dollar is only worth about half of the American dollar. If Yip Harburg was Canadian, when he wrote "Brother, Can You Spare a Dime?" he would have had to have called it "Brother, Can You Spare a Quarter?" Everything rhymes with dime. Fine, lime, mine, time, vine, wine. The only thing that rhymes with quarter is "shorter." How great a song would that have been?

Rather than

Say don't you remember they called me Al
It was Al all the time
Say don't you remember they called me Al
Brother, can you spare a dime?
It would have been
Say don't you remember, they called me Al
Just like Allen only shorter
Say don't you remember they called me Al
Brother, can you spare a quarter?

Well, that did it. From that point on, we were friends.

I generally like to keep something from everybody I worked with to remind me of them, so when I was taking him to the airport a few days later, I said, "Sammy, I'd love to have a keepsake to remember you by. Do you have a publicity picture or some such?"

"I don't have anything to give you," he said. "But let me get back to New York and I'll send you something."

A week later, an envelope came to Kramer Management. I don't know what it was. I opened it and there was a heavy piece of cardboard. I turned it over and it had a bunch of Canadian coins taped to it, and underneath it said, "To Marty, this is for you. Sammy." On the front, there was an 8 x 10 of Sammy and his keyboard and through the keys, it said, "To Marty Kramer, future Hall of Famer, you made my stay in Vancouver groovier." It was signed by Sammy Cahn.

You can keep your first editions of Hamlet. That is one of my most prized possessions.

20

THE DEVIL WENT DOWN TO GEORGIA - AND HE SCORED

Over the years, I've had a number of interactions with non-music world celebrities such as Chuck Norris, and Jimmy Connors to name just a couple. Often these encounters were precipitated by nothing more than some producer's whim of the moment.

We were shooting an episode of *The Paul Anka Show* and the producer came to me and said, "The Oilers are in town. Why don't you see if you can get Wayne Gretzky to appear on the show?" My answer was, "Gretzky can't sing. What are you going to do with him?" His response was, "Leave that to me. Just see if you can get him."

I tracked Gretzky down and somehow managed to convince him to return with me to the studio. I put him in the dressing room next to my office and went to inform the producer that Gretzky was there. The producer handed me a small cassette recorder and said, "'The Devil Went Down to Georgia' is on there. Have Gretzky learn the lines."

I repeated what I had said earlier that Gretzky didn't sing but the producer just said, "He doesn't have to. He's going to lip-synch the song. Don't worry. The band will be playing and most of the time the camera won't be on him so if there's any problem, we'll edit it out. Just get him to learn the lines."

I went back to the dressing room and even though Wayne thought it was crazy, I got him to learn the song and left him to practice in front of the mirror. Half an hour later I returned with the producer who took Wayne off to the taping. As it turned out, Wayne was great, and it all went off like clockwork.

Once the taping was finished. I drove Wayne back to the arena for his game that night. He was in fine spirits, quite happy with how everything had gone. I guess when you're used to 25,000 people screaming at you, and four superb athletes trying to drive you into the boards at thirty miles an hour to turn out your lights, lip-synching "The Devil Went Down to Georgia" is no big deal. Come to think of it, given the choice between the two, I'd lip-synch the song on live television dressed only in my underwear.

21

BURGERS WITH BILL

It was the mid-90s and I was looking after a road tour for Randy Bachman. Generally speaking, Randy wasn't big on tours, preferring to play in small venues. Occasionally, as when he did the *Ringo Starr and his All-Starr Band Tour* he would play for large crowds, but he liked to keep these to a minimum. Randy was a shrewd businessman and didn't require the income generated by tours. He controlled all his own publishing which is the most lucrative part of the music business. Which is what led to the decades-long dispute between Randy and Burton Cummings. Originally, all the publishing of The Guess Who was owned and controlled by their producer Jack Richardson. Richardson was legendary, having mortgaged his home to record The Guess Who's initial hit album *Wheatfield Soul* at Phil Ramone's studio in New York, and then went on to produce hits for artists such as Bob Seger, The Irish Rovers, Alice Cooper, Bad finger and Poco among others.

In the late 70's, Richardson ran into financial problems, and the publishing was put up for sale and acquired by Burton. Randy alleged that he wasn't aware that the publishing was available and if he had been, he would have acquired it which was the beginning of the great Bachman-Cummings War. But more of that in another chapter.

We were headlining a state fair in middle America, I believe the Spirit of Chicago. We were at the fairgrounds at the performance stage, and I was doing sound checks and setups and Randy was rehearsing his set. There were all sorts of rides and a food area around us, and we were in the center. I looked over my shoulder and noticed a procession of black Chevy Suburbans approaching. They were all flying American flags. They stopped not far from the stage and then a phalanx of Secret Service personnel got out of the limos followed by President Bill Clinton and started walking in our direction. I remembered seeing the President playing the saxophone and I always suggested we should include a sax in "Takin' Care of Business." I ran over to Randy and told him to start playing "Takin' Care of Business," and I turned up the volume. This was around the time that Randy had licensed the song to Office Depot for their radio and TV ads and it was impossible to go a day without hearing the song at least three times somewhere.

I ran back outside and as the group passed close to us, I shouted out, "Hey Mr. President, I'm the tour manager for Randy Bachman and we're doing a show here tonight. If you happen to have your sax with you, why don't you join Randy on stage tonight for "Takin' Care of Business?" Bill laughed and shouted back, "I'd love to, but I didn't bring my saxophone. I'm just heading over to cook hamburgers for these folks. Come on over and I'll make you one."

After we finished the setup and sound checks, Randy and I wandered over down the midway to where the President was making burgers. There were a couple of hundred people standing around where he was working the grill. We gradually made our way through the crowd and when we reached the front, the President smiled and greeted us. He was wearing an apron and flipping burgers and offered to make us a burger which we accepted. He put together cheeseburgers for both Randy and me and said, "Enjoy." Now I can hear you say that technically, that wasn't exactly having dinner with the President. But that cheeseburger was my dinner. And the President did make it for me. And admittedly, other than occasionally sampling one of the burgers, he wasn't eating. Still, under the rules of artistic license, I feel I'm entitled to claim I had dinner with the President. Nowhere is it written he had to have eaten a meal or been sitting or that there were just the two of us?

I'm sure there are occasions now when he and Hillary are sitting in front of the fire reminiscing about the old times, and he will say, "Did I ever tell you about the time I had dinner with Marty Kramer?"

22

IT'S A SMALL WORLD

Sometimes my interaction with celebrities was nothing more than momentary. I was at the Four Seasons Hotel and saw Michael J. Fox. Of course, I went over and introduced myself. I said, "I'm Marty Kramer, the tour manager for The Guess Who. I'm a big fan of yours." He thought for a moment and then said, "Of course. 'Clap for the Wolfman.'" (One of The Guess Who's big hits.). Michael pulled a *Back to the Future* card from his pocket and signed it "Go Marty Go" and gave it to me.

End of story. I told this to my friend and co-author David and said, "My contact with Michael J. Fox was vicarious. Do you think we should even include it in the book?" He laughed and said, "You think your contact with Michael J. Fox was vicarious? Let me tell you mine." And I'll let David finish the story.

It was 1982. A friend of mine was a senior A & R rep at one of the majors when he was approached by a group of Japanese investors who wanted to start their own record label and hire him as President. They were prepared to fund the label for a minimum of three releases. They had two groups they wanted to sign but would leave the third up to my friend. He wasn't impressed with their choices, but he had a group he knew was great that he wanted to sign, and so he agreed.

They recorded the first two albums with the investor's groups, and the albums died faster than the guy who walks into the garage in a horror movie and says, "I'm not afraid of any dumb ghost." My friend finished recording the album with his artist, a local singer by the name of Billy Vera, and his group, The Beaters. Before it was released, he sent me a copy and asked my thoughts, as I was heavily involved in the music business. I told him that in my opinion, it was mostly just what we called album cuts, but there was one song, "At This Moment," which was a monster and would make his label, so he needn't worry. He told me he agreed, but the investor's other two groups had already tanked, the investors insisted he release one of the other Billy Vera songs first, which they did. And the album died faster than you can say in Japanese: "Stay the fuck out of the music business if you don't know what you're doing."

The money was gone, and they weren't prepared to invest more, so the label folded before "At This Moment" was released as a single, and the masters were sold to a small local record label, Rhino Records for a few thousand dollars.

We now go to three years later, and my friends Al Blye and his wife Rita Rogers who live in L.A. Al was the brilliant producer of such TV hits as *The Sonny and Cher Show*, *The Smothers Brothers Show,* and a dozen others. Later, in the 80's he had the Showtime hit, *The Super Dave Show* with the great Bob Einstein, probably one of the funniest shows ever to grace TV. I was privileged to be part of the group that put that show together and was one of three credited writers in season one. Apropos nothing, Bob Einstein was a lovely man, and one of the funniest comedians of the past hundred years, and sadly passed away a short time ago.

In any event, in 1985 Rita was the director of the hit TV series *Family Ties* starring Michael J. Fox. They were shooting the final show of the season, and Michael's character Alex was standing in the train station as the love of his life Ellen (Tracy Pollan) was leaving him. Rita needed a song to play over the dramatic scene and she remembered having heard Billy Vera perform "At This Moment" at an L.A. club. She sourced the record from Rhino, a small novelty and reissue label, signed a licensing deal, and included it in the soundtrack. Immediately after the show aired, switchboards at NBC local stations lit up with fans demanding to know where they could get the record. Rhino re-released the album. "At This Moment" went to the top of the charts, number one, and remained on the charts for 21 weeks. It made Rhino Records which is now the Rhino Entertainment Group, the catalog division of Warner Music Group.

A relationship with Michael J. Fox doesn't get any more vicarious than that. From me to a group of amateur Japanese investors to my friend setting up a label that went bankrupt to a small reissuing label acquiring their catalog to my friend Rita having heard a song in an L.A. club that perfectly fit her needs and remembering it at the right moment to Michael J. Fox. That, my friends, is show business.

23

MY DINNERS WITH RODNEY AND JACKIE

My clients were mostly limited to the world of music. On occasion, however, I was called upon to work with other genres in the business.

I had just finished the last leg of an international tour and was tired and getting ready to head back to the West Coast for a little R&R when I received a call from a promoter friend of mine. He had Rodney Dangerfield coming to town for a one-night performance and wanted me to look after him. This business is built on relationships, so I of course said I'd be happy to oblige.

I was waiting at the airport when he arrived and as was my custom, I introduced myself saying, "Mr. Dangerfield. I'm Martin Kramer and I'll be looking after you during your stay." I was always formal unless asked to be otherwise. He said, "Call me Rodney." And so I did.

We were waiting by the luggage carousel for his bag when he said, "That's mine." There was a large trunk balanced at the top of the carousel which then came shooting down the slide like it had been launched from a cannon and crashed onto the rotating carousel. I went running after it and with a great deal of effort, managed to extricate it and get it onto the ground. It must have weighed eighty pounds. I took Rodney and his trunk to my town car and headed into the city. I offered to drop him and the trunk at his hotel and pick him up before the show, but he declined, saying, 'By the time I get there, it will almost be time to leave. Let's just go to the theater and I'll go to the hotel after the show." So we did.

I got him settled in his dressing room and then went to attend to the various sound and lighting checks I carry out before every performance.

It was now 5:30 and the show didn't start until 8:00, so I went to his dressing room and asked if there was anything he'd like to do before the show. He said that he'd like to have a bite to eat and asked if I'd care to join him for dinner. I said I'd love to and named several restaurants that were close to the theater and offered different types of cuisine. He said, "How about we just eat in my dressing room." I said that would be great and I'd get several take-out menus from my office, and he could choose. He said, "That won't be necessary. Did you get what I asked for in my rider?" I said I had, but all that he had asked for was a loaf of rye bread, a pound of butter, tea, condiments, a knife, and some plates and napkins, all of which I had set up in the small sitting room adjacent to his dressing room.

He said, "That's all we'll need." He then opened the trunk and there were a few clothes, some toiletries, and a large plastic Ziploc bag. He pointed to the bag and asked me to bring it into the other room which I did. It must have weighed 40 pounds. I laid it on the table. He opened the bag and in it were many, many dozens of cans of sardines. Some with peel-back tops, and others with those little keys you insert and roll back the top.

He said, "They're the best. I get them from all over the world, Finland, Norway, Denmark, everywhere. Some are in water, some in oil. I prefer them a little spicy, like with a tomato sauce. How about you?" I said, "I usually prefer just water." He said, "Good. I hate them in just water."

And so we buttered some bread, spread some sardines, and had sardine sandwiches. For the next two hours, we talked about his early life and his time on the road. It turned out we had both come from relatively poor homes. His father deserted the family early on and was rarely home. I was an orphan. Somehow, we had both made our way into show business. I hate sardines, but it was one of the best meals of my life. After the show, I packed up his trunk and delivered him to his hotel. The next morning I picked him up and took him to the airport. I got him and his trunk to the check-in counter and then I shook his hand and told him how much I had enjoyed meeting him. He smiled and said, "I know I'm probably the only person in the world who likes sardines. Was it worth it to have to eat sardine sandwiches?" I said, "I'd take my dinner with you last night over a month of meals at Sparks Steak House in New York any time." He patted me on the cheek and said, "I like you, boychick." And then he was gone.

Rodney passed away in 2004. His headstone reads, "Rodney Dangerfield. There goes the neighborhood." What I wouldn't give for one more sardine dinner with that great man.

It wasn't long after that when I was asked to look after the legendary Jackie Mason during his one-week engagement. I picked him up at the airport, and again, as was my practice said, "Mr. Mason, I'm Martin Kramer and I'll be looking after you." He said, "Call me Jackie." Which I did.

On the way to his hotel, he asked me if there was a good deli in town and I told him there was a great one, right across the street from the theater. He said, "Perfect. At some point in the week, we'll go there for dinner."

For most of the week, I took him to and from the hotel and did my usual sound and light checks, but nothing else was required of me. He usually had a small dinner in his room before heading to the theater and the rest of the time he was on his own. I was available to take him anywhere he wanted to go but he really didn't need any assistance. And the rider for his dressing room was just tea, coffee, and water. No sardines. So nothing to worry about there either.

On the last day of his engagement, Jackie said, "After the show tonight, we'll go to the Deli. My lady friend is coming in, so there will just be the three of us." I said I'd look after everything.

I went across the street to the Deli and located the manager. I explained that Jackie wanted to come over after the show, but we wanted a private table where he wouldn't be bothered. The manager was thrilled to have him and showed me where we'd be seated, which was his personal table, separated from all the others. It was a large restaurant, so I walked through. I usually do site visuals when I do shows. I located an exit where Jackie could enter without going through the takeout section or the waiting area and arranged with the manager that he would be there to open the door for us at exactly 10:45.

Jackie did a bit in his show about Carnegie Deli in New York. After attending a Broadway show, a group of non-Jews go to the Carnegie Deli. One of them orders chocolate cake. When the server brings the cake, the rest of the table looks at the huge slice and thinks it's so big it must have been pre-ordered for a special occasion and starts singing Happy Birthday. Shortly thereafter, a group of Jews walk in and one of them orders the same cake and the server brings him an identical piece. He looks at it and then says to the waiter, "The slices are getting smaller and smaller." Such is the Jewish curse. For non-Jews, food is sustenance. For Jews, it's an event.

Knowing my customer, I arranged with the restaurant manager for what I call a Bar Mitzvah table. I told him I wanted everything on the table when we arrived. I explained that Jackie would be tired after the show, leaving early the next morning, and wouldn't want to wait around for the food, so everything should be on the table when we arrived. I wasn't concerned with the cost as I'd barely dented the float I'd set aside for things like meals and entertainment and left my credit card with the manager along with very specific instructions.

After the show, Jackie, his lady friend, and I walked across the street to the exit door where the manager was waiting for us. We were led to his private table which was set out exactly as requested. A terrine of matzah ball soup, plates of gefilte fish, chopped liver, herring in sour cream, knishes, blintzes, pickles, corned beef, salami, cheesecake, rice pudding and every other delicacy a Jew could fantasize about. Jackie was thrilled. Over dinner, Jackie told me he would be in New York the following year in a Broadway production and told me if I was able to be in town at the time, I had to call him and let him know. At the conclusion of the meal the manager came over to return my credit card and let us know that it was an honor having Jackie as a guest and there would be no bill. I left a large cash tip for the servers and then took Jackie and his lady friend back to their hotel.

A year later I was on vacation in New York with my girlfriend and saw that Jackie's show was playing on Broadway. I called the theater and asked to speak to Jackie's publicist with whom I had previously spoken. I mentioned I was in town and just wanted to say hello to Jackie. She insisted I come to the show that night. She said she'd have tickets at Will Call for me along with an invitation to come backstage after the show. Our tickets were for the VIP section and the show was wonderful. After the show, we went backstage and spent fifteen minutes schmoozing with Jackie. We probably could have stayed for another hour, but I knew he should get back to his hotel and get some rest, so we thanked him and left before we overstayed our welcome.

Let me tell you some things about Jackie Mason that you may not know. At age 18 he became a Cantor and at age 25 he was ordained a rabbi, just as three of his brothers, his father, grandfather, and great-grandfather had been before him. In 1953 he graduated with a Bachelor of Arts degree with a double major in English and Sociology from the City College of New York. He served as a rabbi for several congregations, but after his father died, he resigned from his job as a rabbi in a synagogue to become a comedian because, he said, "Somebody in the family had to make a living."

Over the years he has gained an iconic reputation and an international following on radio, television, film, stage, recordings, and as a literary figure. He appeared in numerous films and television shows, including nine appearances on *The Simpsons*, the last being in 2018. He had five television specials, 13 records and DVDs, nine one-man shows, 4 books, and over 200 self-written video blog entries on YouTube. He was also the recipient of several Emmys and a Tony. At 88, he was more in demand than ever, although he was selective in what he accepted. A friend of David's held an eightieth birthday party in Los Angeles and thought about bringing in Jackie to entertain his guests. He inquired as to Jackie's availability and cost and was told Jackie would do a one-hour show for $100,000 plus a private jet to and from New York. Not too shabby for an 88-year-old comic.

Now all of that is public knowledge. But since ostensibly you've shelled out hard cash for this book, let me tell you something that isn't public knowledge. In private, Jackie was the same person you would see when he performed. He was a Jewish Voltaire with incisive opinions on anything and everything that were both thoughtful and humorous. He was warm, gracious, unassuming, and considerate. He'd ask your opinion and then tell you what you should be thinking. Once a rabbi, always a rabbi.

24

Another Short Story (About the Mickey Who Wasn't the Mouse)

I would imagine that it's likely that anyone under the age of fifty may be unaware of the name Mickey Rooney. Rooney was an American actor, vaudevillian, comedian, producer, and radio personality whose career spanned nine decades until shortly before his death in 2014. He appeared in more than 300 films and was the last surviving star of the silent film era. For several years he was the top box-office attraction in the world and subsequently became a celebrated character actor. Sir Laurence Olivier once said he considered Rooney "the best there has ever been." Cary Grant called him the most talented man in the history of movies. Tennessee Williams said, "There is only one great actor in the United States, and that is Mickey Rooney." And Gore Vidal said, "He sings. He dances. He can make you weep, he can play tragedy, he can play comedy….. He's formidable. He can do anything, and effortlessly."

In the early eighties, he returned to Broadway to star in *Sugar Babies* with former MGM dancer and leading lady Ann Miller and again became a celebrated star. The show lasted 1208 performances in New York and then went on to tour nationally for five years including eight months in London, with Rooney never missing a performance.

A diminutive man, barely five feet two inches, Rooney was never concerned with his stature, titling his memoirs *Life is Too Short*. Nor did it ever diminish his social life, having been married eight times, including initially to a woman considered one of the most beautiful women in the world, Ava Gardner who later went on to marry Frank Sinatra.

I had the honor of being Mickey's body man at one point in his national tour of *Sugar Babies*. He was staying at the Four Seasons and when I picked him up, he was accompanied by an older man, Al Stern who it turned out was the doorman from his building in New York, an old friend that he brought with him. When we arrived at the theater, I gave his buddy a gig. I told him, "You stay at the door and check everyone who comes in." which seemed to please both Mickey and his friend.

We went into the theater, and I was taking Mickey to his dressing room when he spotted Ann Miller on the stage conducting the dancing girls in rehearsal. Mickey said, "That looks like Ann on stage. Let's go and say hello." We went to the wings, and I showed him the stairs to the stage. Ann was going one, two, three, kick, one, two, three, kick and didn't see Mickey until he was standing right beside her. The acoustics were great in the theater, and you could hear everything. She stopped the orchestra, looked at him, and he at her. Then he said, "Ann" and she said, "Mickey" and gave him a big hug, and then she said, "You smell wonderful. What's that you've got on." Without missing a beat, Mickey said, "I've got a hard on and I didn't know you could smell it."

The girls in the chorus broke out laughing. Ann Miller turned red as a beet and said, "You think that's funny? Try 10 minutes at triple time until I tell you to stop." The orchestra starts not at 33 or 45 but at 78 speed and they're going a hundred miles an hour without stopping, and she went to her dressing room and wouldn't come out. Which was surprising since she shouldn't have been surprised, having once remarked that, "Mickey never missed a chance to ad-lib or read the lines the same way twice, if he even stuck to the script."

Vanity Fair called him "the original Hollywood train wreck." He was a degenerate gambler, struggled with alcohol and pill addiction, and earned and lost millions during his career—once even filing for bankruptcy. But for a man barely five feet two inches, he was a monstrous talent who lived his 93 years like a giant and was one of the most unassuming, open, generous celebrities I ever had the pleasure to work with, and although he was the supreme prankster, it was always well-intentioned. And he truly loved women. And they loved him.

In his autobiography *Life Is Too Short*, Mickey wrote about how on the opening night of *Sugar Babies*, the audience gave him a 24-minute ovation during which he cried with joy, and then repaid the audience by performing a comic striptease right down to his bright-red long johns. Those long johns became somewhat of an iconic symbol for him, and when he left, he gave me a pair of them to remember him by. I know it sounds a little strange to say that I treasure another man's long johns, but I really do.

25

Guess Who's Coming to Dinner

It was 1999 and my friend and co-author David together with Jack Harper oversaw the opening and closing ceremonies for the upcoming Pan American Games. Jack was one of Neil Young's oldest friends and a member of his original band and David was a prominent entertainment attorney. David's company had produced Russell Crowe's first North American film, For the Moment, thanks to the prescience of David's friend and client Kim Johnston. And David represented any number of musical artists such as Fred Turner of BTO and Burton Cummings from The Guess Who.

Inasmuch as the games were being held in Canada, David thought it would be a great idea to have a Guess Who reunion performance as the headliners for the closing ceremonies. The Guess Who was the most successful rock group to ever come from Canada with both Randy Bachman and Burton Cummings as the lead members of the group, who between them had sold more than 50 million records. Unfortunately, Randy and Burton had not spoken for 25 years and there had been a great deal of unpleasantness and litigation between them over the publishing rights of The Guess Who. Inasmuch as Burton was the less aggrieved of the two, David contacted Burton's manager and proposed the idea, which was immediately rejected. David refused to give up, however, and over the next number of months, he enlisted the help of the Premier of the Province who wrote the members of the band requesting that they put aside their grievances and reunite out of loyalty to their birthplace. This ultimately turned the trick and the band reunited for the one occasion and were spectacularly well received. Although they played the performance together, there was little other interaction between the two principals, each of whom had their own tent prior to the performance.

At the conclusion of the games, David went to work on Burton's manager, suggesting it was time to put aside old enmities and get together for a reunion tour. Part of the problem was that neither Burton nor Randy owned the rights to the name The Guess Who, the same having previously been acquired by Jim Kale, a band member. David persisted however and finally arranged a meeting of all the principals. Fortunately, Jim Kale's lawyer was a partner in David's law firm which helped substantially. After lengthy negotiations, it was finally agreed that the band would reunite for a tour with three of the original members, Randy, Burton, and drummer Garry Peterson. Two other members who had been with the band at one time or another, Donny McDougal and Bill Wallace also came on board as hired players. Jim Kale wasn't in a position health-wise to participate in performing but retained a financial interest.

At the beginning of May 2000, the band got together at a facility called the Transcona Supper Club where they were to rehearse for several weeks before going out on the road. A few days into the rehearsal, Burton and Randy were still not speaking other than when absolutely necessary. Then one afternoon, Randy began to play a new extended riff for "American Woman" that he had composed. Standing in front of the stage, Burton got down on his knees and began bowing to Randy and said, "Nobody in the world can play like you." Randy smiled and said, "And nobody in the world can sing like you, Burt." They hugged and thus ended the twenty-five-year war. They went on to tour successfully for 5 years and a few years after that, Randy and Burton toured together as Bachman Cummings.

I was of course the road manager for these tours, and I remember at the start of the initial tour, I was concerned about the well-being of the guys. They weren't youngsters anymore and for consummate performers like Randy and Burton, two hours on stage is an extremely strenuous and tiring exercise. Moreover, throughout his career, Burton was always wired after any performance, and you couldn't even talk to him for several hours and he never went to bed after a performance before 6 a.m. So I had arranged to hire the best masseuse in the city to be backstage after the performance, should any of the guys want a relaxing massage. After the show in Calgary, she walked up to Randy and asked if he wanted a massage. He said, "Sure. But please look after Burt first. He needs it more than I do."

Playwright William Congreve knew what he was talking about when he wrote "Music hath charms to soothe the savage beast."

26

SILENCE IS GOLDEN - AS IS MR. T

One of my principal rules in dealing with celebrities has always been: Respect the person, respect the moods.

It was 1982 and Laurence Tureaud, aka Mr. T was in Vancouver for a TV appearance and to shoot some scenes with Sylvester Stallone for *Rocky III*. I was assigned as his driver, as well as Stallone's and we had a very pleasant time. Mr. T was friendly and charming and we chatted about various things. When his shooting schedule finished, I picked him up the following morning in my town car. He was wearing what must have been literally twenty pounds of gold chains and jewelry. I placed his luggage in the trunk, and he said, "We're going to the airport. My flight leaves at 3." I said, "If it doesn't leave until 3, why are we going now?" and he answered, "My flight leaves from Seattle." I said no problem and we left.

Once on the road, Mr. T said, "Marty, I'm going to meditate, so please, no radio, no conversation, no windows down." I replied, "I totally understand, but you'll have to say something when we get to the border. Do you have your passport?" He said, "No problem. It's in my bag. I'll get it at the border."

An hour later we arrived at the border. I pulled up and lowered my window and the border officer asked, "Where are you going and who's with you?" I replied, "I'm driving Mr. T. He's in the back and I'm taking him to the Seattle Airport." The border officer said, "Lower the back window."

I turned to Mr. T and said, "I'm putting down the window. He wants to see you." And I lowered the window.

The officer leaned in and asked for Mr. T's passport. Mr. T got out of the car, went to the back, retrieved his passport, and handed it to the officer. Meanwhile, other cars in other lanes were passing by, honking their horns at Mr. T, waving and shouting, and other people were starting to congregate around us. Then the supervisor arrived to find out what the fuss was all about, saw Mr. T, and said, "I'm a big fan. Don't go away." And rushed away to get a pad of paper, returned, and asked for an autograph.

I saw where this was going, so I stepped in, took the pad from the supervisor, and said, "Mr. T has to be at the Seattle airport in less than 3 hours, but of course, he'll sign an autograph for you." I gave Mr. T the pad, he signed, I handed it back to the supervisor who then said, "Everybody, let Mr. T go. He must get to the airport." And we were gone.

Not another word was spoken until I pulled up to the curb at the Seattle airport, turned, and said, "We're here." Mr. T reached into his carry-on bag, pulled out a paper, and scribbled a note that read, 'To Marty. Be Cool Mr. T', smiled and left.

Often with celebrities, it's as much about what you don't say as about what you say.

27

THE ONES I HOPE TO NEVER SEE OR HEAR FROM AGAIN

I imagine at this point you're probably saying "Is this guy living in a parallel universe? Everybody he encounters is a terrific person. What happened to all the slime balls the rest of us hear about?"

In my defense, let me make two points:

1. If you're starting a trial and you hope to win, you don't criticize your lawyer. If you're going in for an operation, you

don't demean your doctor. Tour/road/concert production managers are like that. If they're good at what they do, your success at what you do is directly tied to them, so you want them happy. And I'm good at what I do, so almost all my artists treated me well.

2. I really like people and get along well with them. It's one of the reasons I was able to collect so much personalized memorabilia along the way. I may be kidding myself, but of the hundreds of artists I've worked with, I'm guessing I could call most of them today and they'd be happy to hear from me.

Sure, there were entertainers I worked with that I was happy never to see again. Since any criticism I might levy will, at this stage of the game just get lost in the morass of his indiscretions, let me cite one, Bill Cosby, as an example.

This was a one-off. Cosby was appearing at an outdoor venue. He wasn't staying overnight, just arriving, performing, and then departing. My responsibilities were looking after production, sound checks, meeting the artist, and getting him to and from the stage. There was to be no meet and greet either before or after the show. Nor were there any dressing rooms. Cosby arrived from the airport in a limousine which I met at a designated area. Cosby exited the vehicle followed by two stunning women and his road manager. I had no idea if the women were part of the show or not, but I led them all to a screened-off part of the stage where Cosby and what it turned out were just female companions would wait until the show. None of them spoke to me and in fact, they treated me as if I wasn't even there.

After I got them settled, their road manager took me aside and said, "I'm going to need something for Bill before the show to help him get up, if you know what I mean." Which he then punctuated by holding the top of his hand under his nose and sniffing. I replied I could look after that for him.

"Great," he said, reaching into his pocket and pulling out a roll of bills, "What's it going to run me in these parts?" and then started counting off hundreds.

I said, "Probably two and a half."

He said, "Two hundred and fifty?"

And I replied, "No two and a half...years." And smiled at him.

That was my last conversation with either him, Cosby, or the women. I got Cosby to the stage and back after to the limo, but it didn't appear that anyone was interested in any further interaction.

Now you must understand. I could have scored an 8 ball in 30 seconds after his request, and probably from within 50 yards of where we were standing. And I could have pocketed a couple of hundred dollars for my efforts. There was nothing challenging about getting it done. And nobody would have known. So my reluctance to accommodate had nothing to do with the difficulty or danger of the request. This wasn't the first time I had received such a request and not the last. Nor did I only receive just requests to obtain drugs. Musicians are remarkably generous and on numerous occasions I was offered drugs. Once in the middle of a national tour, a famous musician called me into his bathroom where he had a series of lines of cocaine on the toilet lid and offered to share them with me. Cocaine on a toilet lid was adopted early on as a cautionary technique allowing the user to flush the product down the toilet quickly in the event of concern over authorities. As with other times, I declined the offer, pointing out that I had to be at my best 24/7 to ensure his interests were looked after on the tour so no offense was taken. He died at an early age from complications brought on by drugs and alcohol, a brilliant career cut short way too early.

My reluctance to participate in the use of drugs or the overuse of alcohol had absolutely nothing to do with morality or anything judgmental on my part. I take the position that everybody is entitled to do what they choose with their own body. Rather, my concerns were twofold. Firstly, you get drugs for one artist or partake in drugs with one artist, word spreads and everybody expects the same of you. Secondly, as an orphan and then the product of a very poor home, I realized at a very early age that I had nobody and no financial strength to fall back on in the event of any missteps. I had to be ready to accept that any train I got on, I'd better be prepared to take whatever chances or dangers the journey might produce, and I'd decided early on that drugs and booze weren't worth the journey, so I just never got on those trains. One doesn't last six decades in this business operating at less than 100%.

This brings me back to stars I encountered who were less than 'fine people'. Of course, there were many. Pretentious, self-absorbed, inconsiderate, degenerate, autocratic, sybaritic, condescending, and a dozen other similar adjectives. But they were in the minority and generally, few and far between. The entertainment world is a community, and if you are part of it, whether as a performer or in what we term a "below the line" capacity, it's like any other family. There may be times of stress, but you work together towards a common goal and try and treat each other with respect. Or at least that was what I encountered. And if I'm wrong, then I guess I got lucky, and I'll be the last one to complain. As they say, ignorance is bliss.

28

THE QUADRUPLE THREAT YOU PROBABLY NEVER KNEW ABOUT

I've always had the highest respect for great musicians, singers, and players. But the ones I've held in the highest regard were the ones who were the total package, who could do everything. Play music, sing, dance, and act. Those are few and far between. Hugh Jackman, Lady Gaga, Cher, Barbra Streisand, Madonna, Frank Sinatra, Jamie Fox, and Beyoncé to name a few. There is one, however, whom I'm guessing you may not be aware of who to me is among the very best, a great singer, a great musician, a great dancer, and a superb actor. I'm talking about Bruce Willis.

Most people are aware of Willis's career on the stage, on television, and mostly in films, stretching over four decades. I first became aware of his other talents in 1987 on an episode of *Moonlighting* when he performed "Good Loving." He sang, he danced, he played the harmonica, and he stole the show in one of a great series' greatest moments. Listen to his performance on "Blues for Mr. D." and you'll hear an amazing blues performance, with great harmonica, and as an added plus, Demi Moore made a brief appearance singing "Bye, Bye, My Baby." His performance of "Devil Woman" is probably one of the best renditions of that song ever with a trademark growl in his voice that you can't duplicate. The great pity is that in a busy career, he only had time to record three albums.

Which brings me to my only encounter with Bruce Willis. We were doing a Hard Rock Café tour and he was in the audience. I spotted him seated with a bunch of people. I went over to him, introduced myself as Randy Bachman's tour manager, and said he was going to be going on soon. I knew Bruce sang so I asked him if he wanted to come on stage and join Randy in "Takin' Care of Business." He did and as always, he tore it up. He was spectacular. For him, I know it was just another night. But for this kid from a small town in the Midwest, I not only got to meet one of the truly great giants of show business, I got confirmation that in addition to being a genius, he was also a great guy, who had no pretentions, was extremely kind, considerate, and generous with someone he didn't know from Adam. A true Renaissance man.

At the time of this writing, Bruce is battling a form of dementia, and alongside his family, much of the world is witnessing his decline with sadness and a great deal of love. Yet, as he has with everything throughout his life, he faces it with dignity and humility.

PRINCE
17 NOV 1988
lovesexy 88
CI
BUILDING
GUEST PASS
The JACKSONS
VICTORY TOUR '84
6
SPECIAL
Lower Press
A
4
BEHIND THE
SCENES
VAN HALEN
FACILITY PASS
NAZARETH
FACILITY PASS
U2 ZOO TV TOUR
JETHRO TULL
TORONTO
ALL ACCESS
ERIC CLAPTON
TOUR '88
VAN
LOCAL/HOUSE/PROMOTER

In the world of entertainment, music, film, and television, there are two categories of people above the line and below the line. Above the line are the names everybody knows, the stars. Below the lines are the technicians, managers, promoters, engineers, and functionaries, without whom there would be no concerts no movies, and no television. The people, like me, behind the curtains that few ever see.

Over the years, I have no doubt that I was on the speed dial for more than 225 legendary artists, but 99.99999% of the public would've had no idea who I was. The same would be said about the legendary, promoters and managers, many of whom I had the privilege of working with over the years.

29

FRIENDS IN HIGH PLACES

I suppose I can credit part of my good fortune to luck, but if I am going to be totally honest, I must credit the fact that in my life I have been privileged to be involved with four of the giants behind-the-scenes talents in the industry, geniuses with whom I had the privilege to work. They are each so accomplished, that I wouldn't even try to list them in any order but alphabetically. They are

Michael Cohl – Michael is a concert promoter, theatrical producer, and touring impresario, one of the best there has ever been. He was the former chairman of Live Nation and now runs S2BN Entertainment with offices in New York and Toronto. Michael was named the Howard Hughes of rock' n' roll by *Fortune* magazine and oversaw tours and related businesses for more than 150 artists including Frank Sinatra, The Rolling Stones, Michael Jackson,

Prince, Stevie Wonder, and U2. I worked for Michael for several years on numerous projects and he was always generous with his time, willing to let me do what I did best, and never failing to express his confidence and gratitude. They were great years and I imagine would have continued had I not decided to move to the West Coast.

David Fishoff – If I had to describe David Fishoff in three words, they would be eclectic, genius, and mensch. He is a sports agent, public speaker, author, producer, and impresario. He co-produced with Mark Burnett Productions a documentary series on his rock and roll fantasy camp. And I was fortunate to work with him when he produced *the Monkees 20th Anniversary Reunion Tour, The Dirty Dancing Live Tour* with Bill Medley and Eric Carmen, *Classic Superfest* with Herman's Hermits, The Grass Roots, The Byrds and Paul Revere and the Raiders and the *Ringo Starr and his All-Starr Band* tour among other projects.

Arthur Fogel – Arthur is now the CEO of the Global Touring division of Live Nation Entertainment and the chairman of the Global Music Group. The organization sells almost 50 million tickets to more than 20,000 events every year and his team has managed four of the top five highest-grossing tours in history, including U2, Madonna, Lady Gaga, and the Police. My office was next to Arthur's when he worked for Michael Cohl, and aside from being one of the nicest men you could ever know, you would never have guessed the extent of his talent. He started out looking after lesser-known bands but quickly expanded his horizons. U2's Bono called Arthur "clearly the most important person in the live music world" in a documentary titled *Who the F**K is Arthur Fogel*. I'm incredibly grateful for his friendship and for having my office next to his, even for just a year. One couldn't help getting smarter just by virtue of osmosis.

Shep Gordon – Perhaps the best known and best of all personal managers, Shep is legendary for his brilliance and ingenuity and was rightfully entitled to call his memoirs *They Call Me Supermensch*. His stable of artists has included such superstars as Alice Cooper, Luther Vandross, Groucho Marx, Kenny Logins, Pink Floyd, the Pointer Sisters, Teddy Pendergrass, Frankie Valli,

> and Blondie. Nor has his client list been limited to entertainers. He created the first talent agency to represent chefs. To quote Emeril Lagasse, "He single-handily created celebrity chefs." His client list has included Charlie Trotter, Emeril Lagasse, Wolfgang Puck, and a dozen more of the greatest chefs in the business. He has partnered with restaurants such as the Tribeca Grill, Carlos 'N Charlie's, Spice Market, and Maui Tacos. He also partnered with Van Halen's Sammy Hagar in Cabo Wabo Tequila and with Willie Nelson to create Old Whiskey River Bourbon. More than anything, however, I believe Shep is best known for his generosity.

I remember when I had my office in Shep's building on Melrose when we were working for a mutual client. One morning I showed up at the building and there was a beautiful new Rolls Royce parked at the curb outside the building. Shep came around and asked everyone to be outside the building at 11 a.m. which we were when Alice Cooper showed up for an appointment with Shep. Shep handed Alice the keys and said, "It's for you, in honor of your selling so many albums." Nor was his generosity limited to his artists. I spent a wonderful month's holiday at his home in Maui. A supermensch of the highest order.

It is through each of these men that I came to be involved with a great many of the celebrities I came to work with. And I consider one of life's greatest gifts to me has been the fact that I can call each of these men a friend.

30

In Mythology, They're Often Referred to as Vampires

During a conversation, one of my more famous artists once suggested to me that agents were an essential part of the entertainment industry. When I asked why he felt that way, he responded, "Where else other than politics or the penal system can someone with no heart find steady employment?"

A little man is seated in a seedy bar in West Hollywood hunkered over a glass of whiskey, with six empty shot glasses in front of him. A stranger approaches and sits next to him. He is somewhere in his mid-sixties with a neatly trimmed van dyke and immaculately turned out in a $5000 suit, silk shirt, and tie. On the tip of one collar and on both French cuffs of his shirt, there is a small red "L" embroidered in Gothic type. He turns to the man and says, "You seem unhappy my friend."

The little man says, "Who can blame me? My luck is like the bald guy who just won a comb. I'm an agent. I was just fired by my agency, and they took all my clients. I went home and found a note from my wife saying she'd run off with my best friend. And the bank just called in my loan."

The stranger smiled and said, "I think I may be able to help you." and handed the little man a card which simply read "Lucifer." There was no phone number or address, just a small red arrow pointing down. The little man looked at the card and said, "Lucifer, as in?" to which the stranger replied, "Yes, as in Satan, the Devil, Moloch, Prince of Darkness, Beelzebub, Mephistopheles, Father of Lies, Lord of the Flies and Antichrist. But if you don't mind, I prefer Lucifer. And like I said, I think I can help you."

The little man thought for a moment and then asked, "How can you help me?"

"Well," Lucifer replied, "if you agree to my terms, you can walk out of here, and within twenty-four hours the five biggest acts in the music business will sign up as clients. Then the five biggest producers in TV will engage you as their agent and finally, the five biggest stars in movies will follow suit and engage you as their agent. You'll open your own agency which will shortly become the largest and most influential talent agency in the business. You will be incredibly powerful and wealthy, and the most beautiful women in the world will all desire you."

"And what are the terms you referred to?" the little man asked.

Lucifer reached into his jacket, pulled out a piece of parchment, and said, "You'll have to sign this document which says that hereafter I will own your soul for all of eternity."

"Let me get this straight," the little man said, "you'll do all of that for me, and I just have to give you my soul for all of eternity?"

"Correct," Lucifer responded.

The little man thought for about thirty seconds and then demanded, "What's the catch?"

In the world of entertainment, when it comes to humor, agents are generally the low-hanging fruit, with the through line being that they have no heart or soul. Truth be told, agents are no different than any other professionals. There are surgeons who will fight to their last breath to save your life and others who will sew you up with a sponge, a scalpel, and their wristwatch still inside of you because they are thinking about their midday liaison with one of their nurses. There are lawyers who will fight for your rights no matter if you have no money and there are lawyers who will ask to check your wallet before they let you into their office. People are people and agents are no better or worse than any other calling. And I've known both kinds.

My first experience with the less desirable kind of agent came when I was still in my teens. I was managing a local band and made the mistake of hiring an agent based on what he said he could do rather than on what others said about him. Freddie maintained he could get us some decent-paying gigs, so I agreed to give him a try. The deal was he would get the gigs, do the promoting, and look after the door, in return for which he would get 50% of the gate. He did, in fact, get us a gig at a small, but good venue that would accommodate about a hundred people. The band was just starting out so that met our needs. The night of the show, the place was full, and I counted around a hundred people. Fifteen minutes before the band was to go on, I went to Freddie who was seated at the door selling tickets, and asked for our half of the gate. Freddie opened the small cashbox in front of him and counted out $46.00. He said that $5.00 was his float so that our half of the gate was $20.50. I pointed out that I counted a hundred people in the room so at $1.00 a head that came to $100.00. Freddie said a lot were probably friends of the band who hadn't paid. I just laughed and told him that my boys didn't play for $20.50 so we were leaving. As he started to sputter about our not being able to do that, I just smiled and told him that on the good side, he would only have to refund $41.00 since based on what he said, only 41 people had bought tickets. He reached into his pocket, pulled out a large roll of bills, and handed me $50.00. A lesson I learned very early and one I took to heart.

Thankfully over the years, I was dealing with major artists and, accordingly, the agents I dealt with were all great and professional. There is a good reason why when accepting one award or another, among the first that the artist will acknowledge and thank will be their agent. Most entertainers are consumed with their craft and have neither the will nor the capacity to do the hard work of looking after everything that an agent does for them, and they know that they are where they are thanks in large part to the skill and toughness of their agents. And there is a huge difference between toughness and lack of heart and soul. Good agents are the samurai of the entertainment industry and the reason that many artists don't end up broke at the end of their careers. And most agents have a terrific sense of humor. I first heard the story about the agent and Lucifer 40 years ago. It was told to me by a great agent right after she landed one of my lesser-known artists an opening spot with a major tour that a dozen other artists were vying for. She had to call in major favors to get it for us, but that's what great agents do. Whenever any of my artists would complain about paying an agent 15%, I would simply reply with "15% of six figures is better than 0% of five figures." They got the point.

31

IT'S NOT ROCKET SCIENCE

You are more than halfway through the book and I can hear what you're thinking: "This joker has the sweetest gig in the world. He makes sure the microphones are turned on and the band gets on stage. Then all he does is schmooze with the artists, get them to autograph pictures for his collection, and then party with the groupies." Now to be honest, when I first started out in the business, that certainly is what I hoped and expected my life would turn out to be. Sadly, my responsibilities as tour/road/ manager generally entailed, at a minimum, the following:

1. Contact artists or bands once the show is confirmed.
2. Hire the band and determine the salaries and per diems for everyone.
3. Compile a tour budget which includes all costs.
4. Compile song lists for each performer and band.
5. Confirm the rehearsal date, time, and place.
6. Contact performers and band and make them aware.
7. Establish the length of sets and running order of performers.
8. Book airfare and hotels as well as rental vehicles.
9. Book rental gear i.e. sound, lights, instruments, and technicians.
10. Make up set lists and tour itineraries for everyone and distribute.
11. Transport performers to and from rehearsals and venues.
12. Arrange for band transportation to and from rehearsals and venues.
13. Advance all shows with stage plots, technical riders & show times.

14. Once we are on the road, contact the venues and the hotels daily to reconfirm everything.
15. Compile rooming lists and distribute per diems.
16. Once at the venue, assign dressing rooms, see about catering, staffing, etc., and conduct the sound check.
17. Deal with the press, media, guest lists, and merchandise.
18. Showtime till the end of the show I'm in charge and always there for the performers, band, and techs.
19. After the show meet and greet with performers and sell merchandise.
20. Tear down, take everyone back to the hotel, and do it again the next day.
21. End of the tour pay everyone, fly or drive everyone home until the next time.

Before you start feeling sorry for me, I will tell you that in every 24-hour day, I will, as a rule, have six hours when I'm free to do whatever I wish. Normally I would use the time to grab a meal, clean up, and, sleep for a couple of hours. As the manager, however, I was my own boss and could use the time however I wished. I rarely bothered with groupies since to enjoy them required that I be awake.

Bottom line, it isn't rocket science, but if I failed to take care of any of my responsibilities, the tour or the concert which was my rocket ship, so to speak, would.....well as the catchphrase says, "Boom goes the dynamite."

32

A Production Manager's Lexicon

The first time I met the legendary Richard Wayne Penniman, a.k.a. Little Richard was when he had been hired to do a fundraiser for a major Arts Theater and they had retained me to produce the show. Being one of the original greats of Rock 'n' Roll and one of its most celebrated and charismatic showmen, I couldn't wait.

My usual duties included ensuring everything went according to schedule, sound checks, lighting, and the works, and ensuring there were no hiccups along the way. Little Richard showed up with his usual retinue of 20 men, nineteen of whom did absolutely nothing and the twentieth who was Little Richard's manager. His manager served at Little Richard's pleasure, and Little Richard's pleasure was fairly erratic, so his manager was always extremely nervous.

The show started and Little Richard started talking about religion and singing spirituals. None of his classic hits. This was shortly after Little Richard had found true religion and had sworn off the Devil's songs. At the end of his performance, he announced that he had gifts for everyone waiting in the lobby, miniature bibles.

That proved to be as popular with the crowd who had paid $125 a ticket to hear "Lucille," "Good Golly Miss Molly," "Tutti Frutti," and "Long Tall Sally" as a president is when he announces he's going to raise taxes on the middle class.

His performance had lasted exactly 60 minutes and he walked off the stage. The head of the Arts Theater walked over to where Little Richard's manager and I were standing and said, "The contract calls for 75 minutes. Get him back out there and have him perform some of his hits or he's not getting paid." His manager was just standing there and didn't know what to do. He turned to me and said, "Richard doesn't do his hits anymore and he won't do an encore. I can't make him. What am I going to do?" I said, "Leave it to me." I asked, "Where's the band?" Richard's manager said, "They went to get a drink." I found them, went up to the band leader, and said, "The manager said to get you. You have to go out and do a medley of Richard's greatest songs." The band leader replied, "In all the years I've worked for him, he's never done that." "I said, "He's doing it tonight. Get out on the stage." Little Richard's band is the best in the business, so they went back on stage and started playing.

I found Little Richard and told him, "The boys are starting to do a medley of the greatest songs you've ever recorded. They're waiting for you." He said, "Now?" I said, "Yes, now." He said, "Okay." He ran back on stage and said to the crowd, "How are you all doing? I want to thank you for staying. This has been a long time coming. Haven't done this since I can't remember when. I hope you enjoy this." And then he starts and goes through the entire catalog, "Bonie Maronie," "The Girl Can't Help It," "Lucille," "Tutti Frutti," "Good Golly Miss Molly," "Long Tall Sally," "Keep A Knockin." He got a long-standing ovation, bowed, and then he was gone. I never saw him again.

If you're a production manager and the words "Can't, won't, doesn't" are in your vocabulary, you're in the wrong profession.

33

Know Your Worth

Years ago, early in my career, I had the pleasure of being the body man for Peggy Lee while she was appearing on a network television show. She was on Capitol Records, and I had most of her albums. After getting Peggy settled in her dressing room, I went to look after a few matters for her.

I had a very good friend, Garry Peterson, who was probably one of the best drummers in rock 'n' roll. The networks always wanted a full house for tapings, so there were usually a few tickets available. I called Garry and said, "How would you and your wife like to come and see Peggy Lee?"

His answer was "Sure, I'd love to come and see her. I played with her." I figured, okay, he was a world-class drummer who had played on dozens of albums, it was likely that he'd played with her at one time or another in the studio or at a live show. So I said, "How did you come to play for her?"

"My Dad knew all of these show people," he said. Garry's father was a drummer and on one of the times his father was on the road, he'd taken Garry with him. Garry was four at the time. He was introduced to Peggy Lee as "the world's youngest drummer" and he ended up playing on stage with her.

On the night of Peggy's show, I went to her and told her there were a few people I'd like to bring in after the show to meet and greet and she said, "By all means."

When I brought Garry and his wife backstage, I said, "Peggy I'd like to introduce you to Garry. He's a drummer who played with you many years ago."

After Peggy exchanged pleasantries with the couple, I said, "Garry has a fond recollection of you."

Garry then asked her, "Do you remember me?"

"I just met you," Peggy replied.

Garry shook his head. "Do you remember an older man bringing a little kid to your show? I was just four years old."

And while he's saying this, I can see in Peggy's face that she's remembering the moment. She smiles and says "You? It's you?" She then gets up and gives him a big hug. They talked for a while, and she definitely remembered. It was a great meeting.

Over the next few days, while we were going to one place or another, Peggy said to me "What is it exactly you do for a living?"

"I manage tours and bands on the road, and I look after celebrities when I'm not on the road." I gave her a list of some of the people I'd taken care of at one time or another, including Yul Brynner, Debbie Reynolds, and Harry Belafonte.

She said, "I may have something for you. I have a home in Bel Air in a gated estate. My chauffeur and assistant are no longer with me and I'm looking for somebody. I have a small house on my estate for the assistant and a Cadillac available for his use. I'd like to offer you that position."

"I'm very honored," I said. "By the way what would the job pay?"

She said in addition to the house, car, and food, I'd get $125 a week. At that point in time I was making three times that *per day*, so I said, "As much as I'd love to do it and be part of what you do, I have to respectfully decline."

The money was part of it, but more than that, I found it hard to even imagine giving up all the people and places I would encounter while touring. And as it turned out, it was the right choice. I was enamored with Peggy, but the fever quickly broke.

5
COLLECTIBLES

As I mentioned earlier, a great deal of my life has been devoted to collectibles. Both for myself and others.

34

HOMER SAPIENS

I'm a collector. Memorabilia, toys, pinball machines, cars, comics, albums, CD's, anything worth collecting. I also collect humorous stories.

Most of the stories I consider worth collecting involve the world I've been fortunate to be part of over the past six decades, the world of musicians, entertainers, and the privileged few. Thankfully, I've been able to dance with them without being subject to all the temptations, tribulations, and vicissitudes that seem to impact the inhabitants of that world. One of my favorite stories involves the young rocker who is driving down Rodeo Blvd. in Beverly Hills in his brand-new Mercedes AMG convertible. He pulls over, parks, and proceeds to open his door to get out, when a truck passes him much too closely and shears off the driver's door.

The truck driver pulls over and rushes back to the Mercedes to find the young man screaming "My Mercedes, my Mercedes, my beautiful Mercedes."

The truck driver looks at him incredulously and says "Who cares about the car? Your arm is missing." The young rocker looks at his empty sleeve, and begins to scream, "My Rolex, my Rolex, my beautiful Rolex."

In the entertainment world, there are many prized rungs on the ladder of success, Mercedes, Rolexes, and houses in the Hollywood Hills. Over the past few decades, however, there are few status symbols that approach the level of being featured on *The Simpsons*. Especially if you have children who might not appreciate what a macher, a big man you are. But when they see you on *The Simpsons*, well that's an entirely different story. You are a hero.

It was in the late 90's and I was contacted by *The Simpsons* management team, and they said they'd love to do an episode featuring Bachman Turner Overdrive and they'd like Randy and Fred to voice their animated characters. Randy and Fred flew down and did all the filming. I remained home if you'll forgive the pun to take care of business. After the shooting, Randy and Fred returned home, wearing the *Simpsons* jackets they'd been presented with, and of which they were prouder than if the jackets were Grammys. I called my contact at the show to thank them for looking after my artists, getting the air date, and the usual other management stuff I do. A week later, unsolicited, a care package arrived from the lady I was dealing with which included all the usual collectibles presented to guest artists, as well as a lovely handwritten note thanking me. What can I say but Cowabunga?

35

My 8 x 10 Room

Most houses have a small room with the dimensions of 8' X 10'. I have a room in my home which I call my 8 X 10 room, but not because of its size.

Over the years, many of the artists and entertainers that I've worked with have been kind enough to present me with an 8" x 10" picture of themselves which they've signed, and as you will note from the subsequent pages, many, many of them have taken the time to inscribe a kind and thoughtful note to me. I have framed each of them and I have hung these pictures on all four walls of my 8 x 10 room. By doing this, every time I walk into the room, I am reminded of the time I was privileged to spend with these great people and, well, you get the picture.

Some of the artists in my 8 x 10 room are:

> Dirty Dancing Tour, Nitty Gritty Dirt Band, Iggy Pop, the Contours (Bill Medley, Eric Carman, Ronny Spector), Poison, Robert Plant, The Moody Blues, New Kids on the Block, George Michael, The Bellamy Brothers, Oak Ridge Boys, Badlands, ZZ Top, BJ Thomas, Judas Priest, Stray Cats, Ted Nugent, Bad Company, Neville Brothers, Donovan, Los Lobos, Nylons,

George Fox, Travis Tritt, Vince Gill, Dr. Hook, Carl Perkins, Ricky Van Shelton, David Bowie, Billy Idol, Shenandoah, Kenny Loggins, Robert Goulet, Tom Jones, Gordon Lightfoot, Righteous Brothers, Waylon Jennings, Willie Nelson, Gatlin Brothers, Iron Maiden, Hank Williams Jr., BTO, Mark Farner and Grand Funk Railroad, Georgia Satellites, Everly Brothers, Rare Earth, Peter Paul and Mary, Harry Belafonte, Andy Gibb, Del Shannon, Tina Turner, Brenda Lee, Dixie Cups, Anne Murray, Ricky Lee Jones, Natalie Cole, Michelle Wright, Sass Jordan, Tammy Wynette, Dionne Warwick, Mickey Rooney, Denzel Washington, Mr. T, John Denver, Joel Grey, Richard Harris, Santo and Johnny, Five Man Electrical Band, Paul Kantor, and Lenny Breau.

I'm sure that many of you reading this are thinking obsessive, narcissistic, or some other 3-, 4-, or 5-syllable words. Who knows, you may be right. But whether I was with them on only one occasion or for a prolonged tour, almost every one of them became friends. And even if you may not get to see your friends on a regular basis, what can be nicer than walking into a room in your own home whenever you like and seeing the smiling faces of so many of your friends?

No matter how much time may have passed since I last saw or spoke with most of them, I'm confident if I were to call and say,

"Hi, it's Marty Kramer," they would say. "Hey Marty, nice to hear your voice. How are you?" The pictures not only remind me of each of them, but they also remind me that I always took care of my artists to the very best of my ability, and they knew it.

36

IF I'D BEEN MAROONED ON AN ISLAND WITH CLAUDIA SCHIFFER

It's an old story and if you've heard it before, I hope you will forgive the repetition. I just couldn't think of a better metaphor to explain what I wanted to tell you.

The story is of course apocryphal and is told of a photo shoot involving beautiful German supermodel Claudia Schiffer. It took place on a yacht in the South Pacific. The photographer doing the shoot was brilliant but to put it mildly, far less than appealing. In fact, he was downright obsequious and despite all his efforts, Claudia was indifferent if not outright hostile to any nonprofessional approaches he made towards her. On the third day of the shoot, a storm came out of nowhere and the boat capsized, and all aboard were lost except for the photographer and Claudia, who were both washed ashore on a deserted island.

Fortunately, there was fresh water, fruit, and vegetables on the island, so they were able to sustain themselves, but as far as any interaction between them, Claudia would only permit the briefest of conversations for the first month or so. After a month had passed, however, Claudia allowed her reservations to relax somewhat and became a little more friendly. By the end of the third month, they had become good friends, and by the end of month four, they had become lovers.

One evening thereafter, they were down on the beach enjoying the sunset, when the photographer turned to Claudia and said, "I've got a favor to ask." She replied "Of course, anything. What do you want?" The photographer said, "Remember when we landed on this island, shortly thereafter one of the wardrobe trunks washed ashore. I was wondering if you wouldn't mind wearing this shirt, tie, and suit that were in the trunk?" Claudia was a little surprised by the request but said, "Of course." And put on the clothes. He looked at her and smiled and said, "You look incredible. Also, if you wouldn't mind, would you wear this fedora that was in the trunk?" Again, somewhat mystified Claudia agreed and put the hat on her head. He looked at her and said, "Perfect. One last thing. When the boat went down, I had this marking pen in my pocket. Would it be okay if I used it to draw a mustache on you?" Well, it was starting to get weird, but in for a penny, in for a pound so Claudia said, "Sure" and he drew a mustache above her lips. He looked at her and said, "Terrific. It's such a beautiful night, why don't we go for a walk along the beach?" And so they did.

After walking for about fifteen minutes holding hands, he turned to Claudia and said, "Would it be okay if I called you Steve?" Claudia didn't know what this was all about, but again decided it was easier to agree so she said, "Okay." They continued walking along the beach for another five minutes or so, when the photographer leaned over, put his arm around Claudia's shoulder, and whispered in her ear "Steve, you're never going to believe this, but I'm sleeping with Claudia Schiffer."

Sometimes it's not enough that great things happen. You've just got to tell somebody.

Over the past five decades, I've been fortunate enough to cross paths with many famous people, and as I told you, many of them were kind enough to provide me with an inscribed 8" X 10" picture to remember the occasion. But along the way, on several instances, some of which involved stories that I've related in this book, but others of which for a brief period there was only a short interaction without any memorable story, some of these individuals have permitted the passing friendship to be inscribed in time by a picture of the two of us together.

What follows is a small selection of photographs featuring a few of the legends, luminaries, and larger-than-life personalities I had the pleasure of crossing paths with. I hope you will forgive my boasting, but quite frankly, I just had to tell somebody.

Andy Gibb of the Bee Gees on the set of *The Paul Anka Show*, where Marty served as production manager

PHOTO: LINDA CHOMAK

Marty with Bobby Curtola, one of his oldest friends

PHOTO: BARRY RODIN

Marty with Canada's rock icons The Band at their 1983 reunion. Marty first met The Band during the 1970 Festival Express Tour with Janis Joplin, Mountain, The Grateful Dead, and Delaney & Bonnie.

Marty with Martha Reeves and the Vandellas

Marty with Lenny Kravitz at the Guess Who reunion, where Lenny performed "American Woman"

Marty with Chuck Norris at the *Dirty Dancing* tour. Marty decided it was better to befriend Chuck than to challenge him to a fight.

Marty with Steven Tyler of Aerosmith during the 1995 Ringo Starr & His All-Starr Band tour

Marty while he was manager and tour manager for Mountain with band members Corky Laing and Leslie West backstage at the Los Angeles stop of the Ringo Starr & His All-Starr Band tour, where Mountain were guest artists

Tour manager Marty with the original Guess Who Randy Bachman, Burton Cummings, Jim Kale, and Garry Peterson

Marty with Donovan during the They Call Me Mellow Yellow tour

Marty and Dionne Warwick at a Paul Anka show

Backstage with Burton Cummings, Margaret Trudeau, Marty, and Eddie Mio (New York Rangers goalie)

Randy Bachman, Burton Cummings, Neil Young, and Marty backstage at a concert when Marty was managing Burton

Marty and Neil Young backstage

Marty with Anne Murray when he was stage manager for her show

Marty with Michael Bublé reminiscing about when they first met when Michael was 17 and Marty was a talent coordinator

Marty and John Entwistle—old friends reunited shortly before John's passing

Marty and Roger Daltrey backstage at Quadrophenia

Production manager Marty with Chubby Checker

Dizzy Gillespie with Marty, production manager for the *227* show tour

Manager Marty with Billy Chapman, Randy Bachman, and Tim Bachman

Bobby Curtola, Randy Bachman, Buddy Knox, and Tommy Sands. Photo taken by tour manager Marty at a Buddy Knox concert just a few weeks before Buddy passed away.

Tour manager Marty with Joe Cocker and Joe's manager during Guess Who reunion tour when Joe opened for the band

Marty backstage with old friend Billy Idol

Marty with Rita MacNeil

Marty with Jim "Jumbo" Martin, former manager of the Guess Who, on August 19th, 1980 —the night of the Alice Cooper Riot in Toronto when Cooper failed to show for his date at the CNE rock festival, which purportedly set off a riot.

37

FOR THE RECORD: A FABLE, OR PERHAPS JUST A COVER STORY

For the first three decades of my life, record albums ruled the music world. Record stores proliferated and became the de facto meeting place for young people. And the moment you walked into one of these stores, you were inundated with album covers, not just in the bins, but on the walls, in racks, and hanging from the ceiling, all vying for your attention. Since there was no such thing as a sampling of the albums, and other than one or two singles from the album that you may have heard on the radio, the only way you could find out how good the album was would be to buy it. Truth be told, it was normal for every record to contain only one or two hits, with the rest being what were termed 'album cuts', good, but not good enough to stand on their own as singles. This meant that to a great extent, the labels relied on the album cover to close the sale. In a 1996 interview, The Who's John Entwistle remarked that the cover of their album *The Who by Numbers* had cost thirty-six pounds to create, (for which cover incidentally John had done the artwork himself), while the cover for *Quadrophenia* designed by Peter Townshend had cost sixteen thousand pounds. On occasion, the cost of album covers, and the interior artwork rivaled the cost of the record itself.

The truly great album covers stay with us over the ages and are what we think about when someone mentions the name of the artists. Covers like The Beatles' *Abbey Road* or' *Sgt. Pepper's Lonely-Hearts Club Band'*, Green Day's *American Idiot*, Pink Floyd's *Dark Side of The Moon*, Fleetwood Mac's *Rumours*, U2's *War*, Nirvana's *Nevermind*, Lou Reed's *The Velvet Underground* & Nico's Andy Warhol cover. My personal favorite was *Cheap Thrills*, Janis Joplin's last album with Big Brother and the Holding Company. The cover was drawn by underground cartoonist Robert Crumb, and I happen to think it's spectacular.

I was reorganizing and cataloging my record albums yesterday. Over the years I have collected one or more copies of every great album and every great album cover. Along the way, whenever I saw a truly bad album cover, I would buy that as well. And while reviewing my albums yesterday I was astonished at how many bad ones there were. Albums like Nancy Walker's *I Hate Men, Great Organ Hits* with Eddie Layton, *Living Marimbas* with Mexican Joe, and Orleans' *Waking and Dreaming*.

But there was one that stood out from the rest and was in my opinion easily the winner.

This morning I went to fill up my truck with gas. I had left my wallet and credit cards at home but had cash. I turned into the self-serve gas station near my house, parked at pump number five, and went into the convenience store to pay. When I got to the front of the line, I laid down three twenties on the counter and said, "$60 on number five." The fellow behind the counter smiled and said, "What race is he running in?" I laughed, filled my tank, and was heading home, still thinking about the album cover, but suddenly in a gambling mood, and the following scenario came to my mind as to how that album must have come to be.

Three of the music industry's greatest executives, Clive Davis, Tommy Mottola, and Ahmet Ertegun are seated in Nate N' Al's Delicatessen in Beverly Hills having lunch. They are discussing great album covers when the conversation turns to truly bad album covers. Every time one such cover is raised, one of the three says "I could have designed a worse cover." Finally, the three agree on a contest. They will adjourn and each of them will design what they believe will be the worst album cover ever, designed to sell the fewest copies. It must feature real people and be music-oriented. They will reconvene in one week and choose the worst of the three and will then incorporate a new label and release the album with the two losers paying all the costs.

A week later the three convene again at Nate N' Al's. They order their lunch and then Tommy reaches into his briefcase, pulls out an album cover which he lays on the table, and says, "Look at the winner and weep." The cover is titled *Amen Brother* and it is ten Elvis impersonators singing Gregorian

Chants. Ahmet laughs and says "Are you serious? Elvis fans will see his name, won't read any further, and will buy it. Then half a million

right-wing religious wackos will think Elvis found religion and they'll buy it. The record will go gold. Here's the winner."

Ahmet reaches into his briefcase and pulls out his album and lays it on the table. It's titled *Coming of Age*" and it's 10 unnamed 13-year-old boys, each singing their Bar Mitzvah maftirs. Ahmet just smiles and says, "Top that."

Clive shakes his head and says "Ahmet, you're a brilliant executive, but you just don't understand Jews. Ten thousand Jewish fathers will claim their son is one of the kids on the album and they'll each buy two hundred copies to give to their friends and family. The album will go platinum. Sorry guys, but here's the winner."

Clive reaches into his briefcase and pulls out the album you see on the opposite page. And it wasn't just a trifecta, it was a superfecta. *The Mighty Accordion Band. The Royal Polka Kings*. No vocals, just instrumentals. And they're wearing coveralls. And if that weren't enough, the coup de grace was the title. 'Touring Manitoba'. Brilliant. If you leave Winnipeg and go as far as you can in any direction while still staying in Manitoba and forget about seeing another person, you'll be lucky to see a moose. 'Touring Manitoba'. That's like saying I'm going to swim the Atlantic hoping to meet people or dig in the Mojave Dessert planning on finding gold. What have you been smoking?

Ahmet and Tommy fold, the album is released, and I manage to buy one of the six copies sold.

I must be totally honest. The runner-up for worst album cover, in my estimation, was also the same Mighty Accordion Band with their album *They Said It Couldn't Be Done – But they didn't reckon with The Mighty Accordion Band'* whose cover features a gorilla sitting in front of a music stand and playing an accordion. Which is probably why that whole scenario came to mind in the first place after the clerk's remark "What race is he running in?" Talk about a daily double.

38

PINBALL WIZARD

Interactive games have come a long way in the past fifty years, starting with Pong and then progressing with such household names as Atari, Nintendo, Sega, PlayStation, Wi, Xbox, and many others. But in the beginning, going back to the late 1700s and down through the ages thereafter, it was always pinball machines. Certainly, there were improvements along the way, with the addition of spring launchers, electrification, bumpers, flippers, solid-state electronics, and digital displays, they just kept getting better and better. But always it boiled down to just one thing, you against the machine.

Growing up, in the summers I would go to a nearby beach and the place to hang out was always the pier and the arcade. Even though money was scarce, I always found enough to play the pinballs, and although never much of an athlete, when it came to the pinballs, I was not too shabby.

Once I began my career in the music industry and started accumulating all sorts of collectibles, one of my highest priorities was pinball machines and over the years I managed to acquire some of the very best and most popular games. I have spent more than I'd care to admit servicing these machines and ensuring they remained pristine, and without wishing to sound immodest, have become more than proficient in my scoring.

I have also acquired a number of arcade video games such as the 1981 Tempest by Atari which was gifted to me by my friend Burton Cummings, and there are nights when I can't sleep when I can be found playing this game for four or five hours, trying to reach the magical level 99, when it stops changing levels and 16 random variations appear to drive the player even crazier. Although Burton is over 1500 miles away, we are always competing on our respective machines to achieve the highest score.

Ultimately, however, I always revert to my beloved pinball machines. And what, you might well ask, has that got to do with the world of music? Well, the answer is simple. I acted for The Who collectively, and for Roger Daltrey and John Entwistle individually. And John was also my friend. One of the most popular songs they ever wrote, and the one performed most often at live performances since its introduction in 1969 was "Pinball Wizard" from their brilliant Rock Opera *Tommy.*

Ever since I was a young boy
I've played the silver ball
From Soho down to Brighton
I must have played them all
But I ain't seen nothing like him
In any amusement hall
That deaf dumb and blind kid
Sure plays a mean pinball

And whenever I play my pinballs, which is often, I find myself singing those lyrics, often not even realizing I'm doing it, and almost always, while I play, my thoughts go to my friend John Entwistle who I'm guessing is looking down from up there and enjoying the action vicariously.

John was the only member of the band with formal music training. In addition to being declared the greatest bass guitarist of all time, John contributed background vocals, occasionally sang lead vocals, played other instruments like trumpet, piano, and bugle, and was a brilliant artist. He was the Leonardo da Vinci of musicians, and when he played, with his amps cranked up to 11, he was in a world of his own. I'm guessing when Peter Townshend wrote Pinball Wizard, he must have had John in mind.

39

THE PAPER CHASE

Long before iTunes, Alexa, and Spotify, before iPhones, Walkman, and Discman, before radio, record players, and phonographs, there was sheet music. Going back more than a thousand years, people recorded their songs by hand and preserved them in manuscripts. This led to what we now call sheet music. Over the years I have collected sheet music, generally what we refer to as 'lead sheets' which just contain the melody, lyrics, and harmony rather than the full orchestration or arrangements. As we move into the digital age, many software products have emerged that have allowed sheet music to evolve into virtual sheet music, or what is termed digital sheet music. Despite this, my collection has continued in the traditional form.

When I met Sammy Cahn for the first time, I believe he was surprised to find out that I knew who he was. Although I never mentioned it, I think he would have been astonished to know that I owned the sheet music for almost every song he'd ever written. And not just his, for most of his contemporaries, people like George and Ira Gershwin, Cole Porter, Jules Styne, E.Y. (Yip) Harburg, Irving Berlin, Lerner and Lowe, Rogers and Hammerstein, and Woody Guthrie. And it didn't stop with his generation since great writers have flourished over the past sixty years. Both *Rolling Stone* and I (out of faux humility, I always list them first) consider Bob Dylan as the greatest songwriter of all time. But right up there with him are people like Carole King, Leonard Cohen, Joni Mitchell, Neil Young, Stevie Wonder,

Bruce Springsteen, Paul McCartney and John Lennon, Paul Simon, Dolly Parton, Mick Jagger and Keith Richards, Brian Wilson, Bob Marley, Kris Kristofferson, Eminem, Loretta Lynn, Elton John and Bernie Taupin, Neil Diamond, Merle Haggard, Billy Joel, The Notorious B.I.G., Willie Nelson, Burt Bacharach and Hal David, Chuck Berry, Ellie Greenwich and Jeff Barry, Jerry Lieber and Mike Stoller, Smokey Robinson, Joan Baez, Roy Orbison, Freddie Mercury, Gordon Lightfoot, and Townes Van Zandt. And that's just scratching the surface. And I've collected them all.

Looking back, I believe my obsession with songwriters began when I was just a teenager. I couldn't sing or play an instrument or read or write music. But there was a moment when I first recognized the power of song. It was when I saw the brilliant 1942 movie and heard the song written by Herman Hupfeld. Don't feel bad if you don't recognize the name. Most people wouldn't. I believe the song in question was the only song he ever wrote that achieved any kind of success. But oh what a song. It set out in a few verses the guidelines delineating most of our lives. The movie was *Casablanca*, and the song, of course:

You must remember this
A kiss is just a kiss
A sigh is just a sigh
The fundamental things apply
As time goes by

And I've continued to collect the written words of all the great songwriters of the past hundred years. Not unlike bibliophiles who love browsing through their books, I can pass hours on end scrolling through my cabinets of written music, plucking lead sheets out at random, and savoring the contents. And when I'm doing that, well, the time it just goes by.

40

UNLIMITED ACCESS IN THE VALLEY OF THE DENIED

Everything in life is relative. You may own a small farm in Nebraska, getting by on the crops you raise and the freshwater well on your property. You may consider your life underprivileged, but there are a billion people in third-world countries with little food who must walk five miles for fresh water to drink and who would look at you as royalty. I could give you a hundred other examples, but you get the idea. It's all relative.

Without getting all philosophical on you, I am bringing this up because of my continuing house cleaning and reorganizing of all my memorabilia. This morning I went through my filing cabinet of backstage and security passes. Like everything else associated with my work, I have kept every one of these documents from my first concert going forward and have several thousand of them. You can see a small number of them on the section breaks of this book.

Why is this important or of interest? In the world of concerts, backstage passes are the ultimate prize. Anybody can score tickets to a concert, but you must know somebody to get your hands on a backstage pass. It's one thing to sit in the audience and enjoy the concert, but it's an entirely different thing after the concert to go backstage, meet the artists, and pretend, at least for the moment, that you are part of that magical world.

Over the years I've looked on my backstage passes much the way a surgeon looks on a scalpel, or a musician looks on his guitar or piano. They are just tools of the trade. I use my own backstage pass to get around to do what I must do, and I use extra backstage passes as a currency to obtain whatever I require for my artists, be it a special instrument, a luxury limo, or whatever. What people won't part with for money, they will often part with for backstage passes.

When I was the production manager for a Simon and Garfunkel concert, I was approached by a friend who desperately wanted backstage passes. I made it a rule never to use them for personal reasons, regardless of how close the friend may be. My friend owned a pool and spa store, so I struck a deal whereby he installed a portable hot tub in Simon and Garfunkel's dressing room, in return for which I provided him with two great seats for the show and backstage passes. To make the hot tub a little more friendly and welcoming, I floated a couple of plastic ducks on the surface of the water. I only mention this in the event I should die suddenly and in going through hundreds of thousands of pieces of memorabilia in my storage facility my executor comes across two plastic ducks with name tags reading Simon and Garfunkel, he won't think I crazier than he already does.

An old friend of David's produced one of Elvis's television specials and told David about Elvis's tour bus driver. Apparently, the bus driver bedded more beautiful women than Elvis or any member of the band. The bus driver was given two backstage passes for every one of Elvis's shows and generally had a choice of a hundred women who were prepared to do anything for a chance to get near the king. They would have slept with Godzilla. The fact that the bus driver wasn't bad-looking didn't hurt. The point was, that backstage passes are, to put it mildly, gold.

So again, why am I telling you this? The answer is simple. It wasn't until I was looking at all my backstage passes recently that I realized that I have lived the most fortunate of lives. Rather than getting behind the scenes at a concert on one or two occasions, I have spent the past fifty-plus years backstage. Not only have I worked and mingled with many of the greatest artists of the past hundred years, but I was also able to do so in a manner never experienced by your normal backstage visitor. My relationship with these artists was informal, outside the scope of performer and spectator, more collegial than business. We would often share meals together, share a joke or a story together, and in almost all cases, I was treated as a friend and co-worker. For almost six decades, as compared to 99.9% of the general population, I have not only been the one-eyed man in the valley of the blind, but this half-blind wanderer has had the honor and privilege of living among royalty and being treated as one of their own, and so I just wanted to take this opportunity to thank all of the artists that I've worked with over the years for the kindness, consideration and respect accorded this poor orphan from the middle of nowhere who had the good luck to be granted a universal backstage pass.

41

KRUZ CONTROL

Whatever the important life event, whether it was

1. That first time you saw your favorite artist perform live; or
2. The concert where you met your significant other; or
3. The Broadway show that changed your life; or
4. The concert or event that motivated you to change how you viewed life and what you wanted to do with your life.

For many of us, there were only two ways to bookmark that event and remind us moving forward what that event meant to us, either an audio recording or a visual representation of the event, namely a framed poster on our wall.

From as early as the first concert I ever attended, I tried to acquire one of the posters used to advertise the event, although that wasn't always a possibility since there was generally a limited number of those available. It was this lack of hard copies that gave rise to an industry, the king of which is, by some strange coincidence, a friend of mine who was born in the same middle of nowhere as I, and musical notables like Neil Young, Burton Cummings, Randy Bachman, Lenny Breau, and numerous others claim as our point of origin. Perhaps it was the cold winters with nothing else to do or just the isolation, but music seemed to play an inordinate part in all our lives.

As brilliantly recounted in all its purple haze glory, Jerry Kruz recalls the genesis of his career in his book *The Afterthought*, which tells how, with the help of his mentor, Bill Graham, impresario and legendary founder of Fillmore East who was responsible for promoting acts such as Bob Dylan, The Rolling Stones, Stevie Ray Vaughan, Joan Baez, CSNY, Santana, Jefferson Airplane, The Doobie Brothers, Robin Williams, The Doors and John Fogerty, Jerry began his journey as founder of one of the nation's first psychedelic music halls which nurtured aspiring music talents to music promoter and ultimately to become the poster king. Along the way, encountering folks like Country Joe and the Fish, Janis Joplin, The Steve Miller Band, The Grateful Dead, Jefferson Airplane, and, of course, Bill Graham, Jerry began what became his ultimate career, acquiring thousands of posters of legendary events.

What most people are unaware of is that amid this life journey, to keep the wolves from his door Jerry took a job in the prison system where he was taken hostage by a gun-wielding prisoner, which still haunts him to this day. But that's a story for another day. What matters is that if like me, you have a framed digital reproduction of an original poster hanging on your wall, chances are it came from the king, my friend Jerry, whether you bought it online, from a music store, or from one of the gift shops in one of the Rock and Roll Museums. With more than a thousand different digital reproductions of his treasure trove of original posters, Jerry keeps our memories of the wonderful world of music alive for us every time we stare at a poster and flashback to that time when our lives changed forever.

6

STORIES BEHIND THE STORIES

42

THESE BOOTS WERE MADE FOR ROCKING, NOT HAWKING

Musicians are no different than any other people, in that like snowflakes, no two are the same. They can be calm or agitated, mercurial or unchanging, passive or aggressive, introverted or extroverted. The great John Entwistle was all of these.

In a musical career that spanned more than 40 years, John was best known as the original bass guitarist of The Who, considered by most as one of the most influential rock bands of the 20th century, credited with originating the "rock opera" and selling over 100 million records. He was nicknamed "The Ox." In 2011 he was voted the greatest bass guitarist of all time in a *Rolling Stone* magazine readers' poll.

It was 1995 and I was on the road with Ringo Starr's All-Starr band. I was the road manager which meant that I had nothing to do with booking the dates but was responsible for ensuring that everything else on the tour went as it should.

As a prelude to this story, let me tell you about John's wardrobe case. It was the biggest trunk I'd ever seen, and it wouldn't fit in any of the dressing rooms on the tour. We could get it in the building without any problem, and roll it down the halls, but that was it. Thereafter it remained in the hall. John was the only one whose trunk remained outside his dressing room. His wardrobe case contained two of everything, jackets, shirts, underwear, boots, the works. At the end of every show, I arranged to turn over whatever he had worn to an assistant who looked after getting everything cleaned.

We were in rehearsal getting ready to begin the tour when I got a call from a guy who said, "We're opening a new Planet Hollywood restaurant in town, and we'd like to get Ringo and the All-Starr Band to perform." I explained that the band didn't do that sort of thing, and at the end of the day Ritchie wasn't interested in any engagements, but I'd run it by the rest of the band to see if they felt like dropping by. The fellows said they were happy to do it, so I set everything up. They'd drop by for a brief meet and greet and then they'd like some privacy for dinner. He was thrilled and agreed.

We showed up, had a brief public appearance, and then were shown to a special VIP area. John, Zak Starkey, and I were seated at one table, and the others who were non-smokers at a separate table beside us. We were having some appetizers and drinks when one of the security personnel approached the table and told us that there were a couple of ladies who'd like to meet John. We looked over and saw two stunning women, so John said, "By all means."

As the ladies were walking over, it became immediately apparent to me that they were both two sheets past three sheets to the wind. They were staggering a little bit and giggling, and I sensed trouble. Before I could say anything, however, one of the women approached John and started to say something, but not watching where she was walking, she stepped on the toe of one of his boots. John leapt up incensed and started screaming at her. Security came back and escorted the women out. We said our goodnights and left.

The next day we we're leaving for L.A. to go to Japan for the opening night of the tour. I got Ritchie and his wife Barbara, and the rest of the band loaded up and headed to the airport. I settled the bill at the hotel and as I was leaving a chambermaid came running up to me and said, "Mr. Kramer, don't leave. One of the guests forgot something." Turned out it was John's boots, the ones the woman stepped on. Whether he left them deliberately or forgot them, I had no idea, but I put them in my bag and headed to the airport.

We got to Japan and settled into our hotel. I checked in with Ritchie who handed me the band's itinerary and said, "Be a good lad and let everybody have these." Which I did. Apropos absolutely nothing, I have to say again at this point that I am absolutely Ritchie's number-one fan in the world, not only because of his incredible talent and the polite and generous way he treats everybody but also because of his manner of speech. He never orders, demands, or otherwise tries to intimidate. He is always incredibly respectful of everyone and an absolute delight to work with and be around.

In any event, I took the itinerary and delivered one to everybody in the band, saving John's for last. I said to John, "Here's your itinerary, and by the way this belongs to you." And I handed him a bag with the boots. He opened the bag, took one look, reached in, took out one boot, threw it against the wall, and then threw the other one at the door and shouted, "Get out."

I gathered up the boots and left, went back to my room, and put the boots in my production box in case he had a change of heart. Others might have assumed that they had done something wrong or that they were in deep trouble, but the thought never crossed my mind. As a road, tour, and production manager, you quickly learn that it's rarely about you. If you do your job and the artist gets upset, there's generally another reason, so I just carried on. Plus John and I had become quite friendly, so I knew I needn't be concerned.

We finished the Japan portion of the tour and headed back to the mainland, and nothing further was said about the boots. We were back in America and a week or so later, John called and asked me to come to his room. He said, "My girlfriend is arriving at the airport. Would you mind going to fetch her? I told her to look for you." I of course said I'd be delighted to look after it.

She arrived and I greeted her. She said, "You're Marty." I replied that I was. She went on to say "Your John's friend. He speaks highly of you. He loves you. Especially when you brought him his boots to Japan." I was having a déjà vu moment of the scene in the room when she said, "You still have them, don't you?" I replied "Of course. Why do you ask?" She said, "John tells me you're a collector. Do you want them signed? They were custom-made for him. He paid $1000 for the boots but he has another pair." I said, "I'd love to have them signed if he doesn't want them." She said, "Great. Now's not the time but leave it with me for a couple of days. I'll let you know."

A few days later, we were at the next venue. I was doing the sound check when she came and got me and told me to bring the boots. She said, "Come with me." We walked down the hallway to John's dressing room. She knocked and we walked in. John said, "What's up." I was carrying the bag with the boots. She said, "John, did you not say to me that you would sign the boots for Marty?" John kept a straight face and looked at the boots. The dent in the toe where the woman stepped on them was still there. He signed, "John Entwistle" on both boots. I said, "You know I'm a huge fan of yours. I love your song

Boris the Spider." (Boris the Spider was one of the first songs John ever wrote and was on The Who's *The Quick One* album. John had been out drinking with Bill Wyman the bass guitarist of The Rolling Stones when he wrote it.) "I know you did the cover for the *Who by Numbers* album." He said, "You know my work?" I replied "Of course I do. I told you I'm a huge fan. I'd be honored if you could draw Boris on the boots." So he turned the boots over, and on the bottom of the right boot he drew a picture of Boris and wrote "Don't think he will ever mend." Then on the sole of the left boot, he wrote "He's come to a sticky end."

As you've probably gathered by now, I'm not exactly shy, so I said. "I'm a big guy on songs. You know Nancy Sinatra had a song "These Boots Were Made for Walking." Would you sign "These boots were made for rocking?" which he did. Then I said, "One of my favorite songs is by Joe South. He had "Walk a mile in my shoes." Would you write "Rock a mile in my shoes." He did. Then he gave me back the boots and looked at me with a straight face and said, "Mahrty (like Ritchie he always pronounced it as if there was an 'h' in it) if I ever see these boots at Sotheby's, I'll sue your ass off." I replied, "John, you know I'm a collector, not a seller." And he gave me a big smile.

John died on June 27, 2002, one day before the first scheduled show of the Who's 2002 U.S. tour. He was 57. On Peter Townshend's website, Townshend and Roger Daltry published a tribute saying "The Ox has left the building – we've lost another great friend. Thanks for your support and love. Pete and Roger." Shortly thereafter, Bill Wyman tagged underneath "The only man who always played on eleven." referring to the fact that most amplifiers only went to 10, but John insisted that his would go to eleven and would normally pump up the volume to that level which made the rest of the band crazy and slightly deaf.

A few years later, I was doing a review of my collectibles for insurance purposes and decided I should get a value for the boots. I called Christie's and described the boots. The fellow I talked to said, "Put them in a box and send them to us and we'll value them for you." I said that I wasn't interested in doing that at this time, I just wanted some idea of the value. He replied that they would probably start the auction at $25,000. Like I told John, I'm a collector, not a seller. I may have lost a friend, but I'll keep what I have, to remember him by.

43

THINGS GO BETTER WITH...

In an industry that's more than any other rife with drug use, my late dear friend can probably be credited with creating the most often repeated phrase in the professional music world.

Not a day goes by that I don't think about and miss my old friend Bobby Curtola.

Most Americans may not be familiar with Bobby's name, even though he had numerous gold records and played in Las Vegas for many years. He was the first Canadian to have an album go gold. His song "Fortune Teller" was an international hit in 1962 selling 2.5 million copies. And between 1962 and 1968 he had continual single and album releases that were immensely popular. During his career, Bobby achieved 25 Canadian gold singles and 12 Canadian gold albums. He also received an Order of Canada in recognition of his humanitarian work, particularly with children's charities. For most people around the world, however, Bobby's most recognizable contribution to culture was the fact that he wrote and performed the jingle "Things go better with Coke" in 1964 for their advertising campaign and was a pitchman for the company. (This was back when "coke was still cola and a joint was a bad place to be." as the great Merle Haggard sang in "Are the Good Times Really Over for Good.")

Bobby and I went back some 40 years, and we remained close over that entire period. I did all of his four wall corporate engagements over the years, and we would speak on a regular basis. He also referred me to several of my clients for whom I produced shows, such as Martha and The Vandellas and Mitch Ryder and The Detroit Wheels. A couple of weeks before Bobby passed away, he received an award from Canada's musical association, the Juno Awards. He called me from the show and said, "Marty, I'm at a table with a bunch of people. I want you to tell everybody here the nickname you gave me." And then held up his phone. I said, "The Ayatollah of rock and rollah." There was huge laughter. The name had stuck with him for forty years. Bobby then said, "God bless you. What's your schedule? I'm coming to Vancouver, and I want to see you. Coke contacted me and they want me to do a promotion and tour for them. We'll talk about it." A few days later I got a call. "Your old friend Bobby Curtola passed away." He'd gone to Edmonton. Had dinner. And passed away that night.

I don't think Bobby would mind my telling the rest of the story. In his biggest hit, "Fortune Teller" he had written:

Fortune teller, will she stay
Close beside me all the way
You have seen it
All in your crystal ball
She's the only love for me

Bobby was on tour in 2010 and met a girl from the Maritimes. Her name was Karyn Rockford. She was from a small town in the Maritimes, and they fell in love, and she became the love of his life. They were together since 2010. In December 2015, she was driving to the airport to fly to meet Bobby who was touring at the time and en route she was killed in a head-on collision. Bobby was devastated and that was the beginning of the end for him. It was six months later that Bobby passed away; I believe of a broken heart.

In a business where egos are as large as the Hollywood Hills, he may have been a music great, and he may have created the longest-lasting most often repeated advertising jingle in the world, but he was always the kid from Thunder Bay, Ontario, humble, caring for others, loyal to his friends and kind to strangers. My only comfort is that I believe he's happily reunited with Karyn.

44

And Now for the Rest of the Story

One of the things that production managers must concern themselves with is artists' riders. These are addenda to the performance contract that provide specific demands by the artist that must be met by the promoter, who immediately turns the problem over to the production manager. Sometimes it's simple things like food preferences, beverages, dietary requests, the number of dressing rooms and how they should be furnished, particulars of their billings in promotional material, and all such incidentals. For example, Paul McCartney, a vegan, insists that any transportation vehicles provided for him should have cloth rather than leather seats.

When I was production manager for a couple of shows for Michael Jackson and The Jacksons, one of the requests in their rider was for a van with a high ceiling to transport them from the hotel to the venue and back. They didn't want a limousine which attracted hordes of fans and reporters. Michael was extremely shy and reclusive, and he wanted to be able to travel back and forth in an inconspicuous manner and nobody looks twice at a van. I had a friend who built custom limos and vans and went to see him. He had just outfitted a van with a bar, mirror, fridge, and wrap-around lounge seating that would be perfect for Michael and the Jacksons and was getting ready to deliver it to his customer. In exchange for four tickets in the VIP section plus backstage passes for the meet and greet, he agreed to let me have the use of the van for two days before he delivered it to his client.

Just as an aside, apropos of absolutely nothing, the Jacksons had a retinue of around forty people with them. Security, other band members, accountants, wardrobe, lighting, sound, and equipment assistants, and a personal chef by the name of Sy Cosis. You can't make that up. Sy Cosis. They also had a driver, Tito Brando. Tito was

Marlon's son, and I should point out, somewhat of an airhead. The only people who rode in the van were Tito who drove it and Michael and the Jacksons.

On the day of the event, the van arrived at the venue and entered through the large overhead door. The door was approximately 300 yards from the stage and the ground floor seating had yet not been put in place. Tito saw the stage 300 yards away, revved the engine, and then proceeded at 40 miles an hour towards the stage, failing to see the barrier fifty feet in front of the stage until the last minute when he slammed on the brakes, swerved to the side, all the while I was watching in horror and envisioning returning a wrecked van to my friend the following day. Somehow, he managed to stop inches from the barrier. The side door opened, and two of the Jacksons fell to the ground, shaken but unhurt.

Michael was seated in the van and belted in so fortunately he was fine. Their manager came running off the stage screaming bloody murder at Tito who said, "Do you know who my father is?" The manager replied, "I don't give a fuck if your father is God's right-hand man, I'm going to—" At which time I stepped in and told the manager not to worry, I'd arrange golf carts to convey the band to and from the dressing room and then quickly got Tito back into the van and away from the stage. Anyway, back to the story.

What is generally considered the strangest request in the business was contained in Van Halen's rider. Their manager, Eddie Leffler had included a provision that a bowl of M&M's was to be placed in the band's dressing room half an hour before their arrival. Under no circumstances, however, were there to be any brown M&M's in the bowl. The caterer had to remove all the brown M&M's and present them to Eddie on his arrival. Most people in the business came to know of this request and its ostensible purpose, namely, to ensure that the promoter and venue read all the terms of the rider rather than just glossing over them. I say ostensibly since here's the rest of the story.

Eddie was a friend of mine and a great guy. In addition to being the manager of Van Halen, he managed the careers of Karen and Richard Carpenter and worked with the Osmonds, Petula Clark, Juice Newton, and Sammy Hagar, among others.

We were on a seventy-city tour. I was the tour manager for Bachman Turner Overdrive (BTO) who were opening for Van Halen, and as I said Eddie was Van Halen's manager. It was around the middle of the tour, and I arrived at our next city before Eddie and his band. The caterer at the venue came to me and said, "Have you seen this?" and showed me the rider with the M&M's clause. I said that I'd seen it many times. He said, "I'll have to assign a chef to do this. I have a good mind not to do it." Wanting to keep the peace, I said, "No problem. I'll look after it." The fact that he knew about it meant he'd read the rider, so I wasn't concerned with disrupting Eddie's procedure. He calmed down however and said he'd look after it.

Eddie arrived shortly thereafter, and the caterer met with him and somewhat begrudgingly, handed Eddie a package with the brown M&M's in it. Eddie puts them in his pocket, just as I'd seen him do many times before.

Later in the day, after we had each carried out our respective responsibilities and we had a couple of hours before the show, Eddie and I slipped away to grab a bite to eat. Over our meal, I mentioned to Eddie about the caterer's displeasure and asked, "Is it really worth it?"

Eddie started to laugh and said, "You mean the M&M's? They're for me. I love the brown ones."

Knowing that the band was more concerned that the cabinet was stocked with Jack Daniel's, Champagne, and expensive liquor than they were about food, I asked, "And does the band care about the M&M's?" Eddie laughed even louder and said, "The band hates M&M's. I throw them out before they get there. Every time."

And that's the rest of the story.

45

ELVIS IS IN THE HOUSE

Over the years, I've managed to interact with almost all the greats of Rock and Roll who were still among the living when I got into the business. Bill Haley, Buddy Knox, Little Richard, The Beatles, The Rolling Stones, Fats Domino, Eric Burdon, AC/DC, The Monkees, Joe Cocker, Neil Young, The Who, Chubby Checker, ZZ Top, Led Zeppelin, The Beach Boys, Rod Stewart, The Eagles etc etc. The one name that stands out as missing, however, is the King, Elvis

Presley. Sadly, Elvis passed away while I was just getting started in the business.

Not to be deterred however, I have managed to make Elvis a large part of my life over the years. I've met members of Elvis's family and his band. My friend Colin Wiebe, a brilliant musician, artist, and tech wizard entered a People's Choice contest a few years ago sponsored by Elvis's estate to draw the best caricature of Elvis, and Colin took first place. For many years, I've brought Elvis to the people with my *Elvis, Elvis, Elvis* tribute review, featuring Shawn Klush and Donny Edwards, the only two Elvis tribute artists endorsed by Elvis's estate. So for all practical purposes, Elvis is still in the house.

The only time our tribute shows ever received less than stellar reviews or an enthusiastic reception was in the early nineties and involved what I generally refer to as "merch" or merchandise. From the inception of my career, I have made merchandise an integral part of any performance I was involved with. Regardless of the artist, when the audience left it was important that they had something to take with them to remind them of the show and ensure they would be back the next time you came to town. Also, it was an extremely lucrative aspect of the business. If the artist hadn't already looked after this, then I stepped up and ensured that it was taken care of. It didn't matter what, t-shirts, mugs, pictures, brochures, posters, caps, CDs, just something they could buy during the intermission or after the show to take with them to remember the event.

On this occasion, I had commissioned Sandy, my t-shirt supplier, and an old friend, to create and prepare for me a few hundred Elvis t-shirts. He had been doing this for me for years, so all I had to tell him was "A caricature of Elvis on the front, some wording on the back, and the numbers of t-shirts in each size." I picked up the t-shirts prior to the tour and they flew out the door at the event and were quickly gone to a greatly appreciative crowd. I was just packing up the merch table when two women came over, obviously agitated and both wearing one of my t-shirts. One of the women started yelling at me, things like "I'm the President of Elvis's fan club. What you're doing here is a complete disgrace. You sold me this shirt."

I had no idea what her problem was but immediately assured her that if she was unhappy, I'd gladly refund her money.

She said, "Do you see what's on this shirt?"

I said, "It's a great caricature of Elvis." Forgetting about what was on the back.

She said, "Tell me you didn't know this was on the back." and she turned around. On the back was written "Elvis is dead. Deal with it."

Then she called over her friend and showed me the back of her shirt which said, "Elvis is dead and I'm not feeling so good myself."

I told her "Give me a minute." And I walked over to where the security guard was standing and told him "Come back with me and just repeat what I say." We went back to where she and her friend were standing, and I said to him "Do you think this is a great caricature of Elvis?" and he said, "What a great picture of the King."

I said, "Okay, now look at the back of these shirts. I think what's written there is funny. What do you think?"

He said, "Absolutely. It's all in good fun." I thanked him and sent him away and then turned back to the ladies.

I said, "I understand that what I think is funny may not be funny to you, so if you're unhappy, I'm more than happy to give you back your money. We're sold out and more people want these shirts than we can supply."

She looked at me and asked, "Do you really think it's good?"

I said, "Absolutely. Let me give you back your money and…"

She stopped me and said "No, it's okay. We'll keep them. You're right. We overreacted." And there was peace in the valley.

When I returned from the tour, I went to see my friend Sandy and told him what had happened. He said, "I thought they were funny. I guess it's good I didn't put on the back what I was originally planning on doing."

He went to his desk and got an envelope which he handed to me. It was a mylar of what was ostensibly Elvis's last prescription.

It was dated August 15th, 1977, the day before Elvis died, and was signed by his physician Dr. George Nichopoulos (Dr. Nick). It was for Dilaudid, Quaaludes, Dexedrine, Amytal, and Biphetamine. Sandy said, "I was going to put that on the back of the shirt under the heading "Just what the doctor ordered."

The minute he said that I had a mental image of me being carried out of the venue on a rail, covered in tar and feathers with the crowd singing *Return to Sender*. I took the mylar and buried it at the bottom of my desk drawer, never to be used.

I should mention that during my travels, I managed to acquire what purports to be a true copy of Elvis's Last Will and Testament. I've never removed it from its wrapping and examined it, since being one of Elvis's biggest fans, I'd be disappointed if there wasn't a paragraph in it reading

"And to Martin Kramer, one of my biggest fans, who said I'd never remember him in my will, Hello Marty."

Long live the King.

46

12,000 Miles – The World's Longest Six-Day Music Tour

It was the early nineties. Ringo Starr's All-Starr Band was performing in Minneapolis. The president of Northwest Airlines was in the audience and after the show, he came backstage and asked to see me. He explained that Northwest was embarking on a major expansion, and was opening hubs in six Canadian cities, Vancouver, Winnipeg, Toronto, Montreal, Ottawa, and Halifax and to promote this, he wanted to sponsor a tour of the band to those cities. I explained that Ringo generally wasn't anxious to participate in those kinds of events, but if the money was right, I could probably put together everybody else, namely:

> **Billy Preston** – Legendary performance and sessions singer and musician with one of the most eclectic histories of any performer. Preston who was one of only five musicians credited on a Beatles record other than the group's four, also recorded with Eric Clapton, The Rolling Stones, Whitney Houston, and numerous other music greats, was the first music guest artist on *Saturday Night Live*, composed Joe Cocker's massive hit, "You Are So Beautiful," and contributed the line "If you can't be with the one you love, love the one you're with" to Stephen Stills' iconic song, just to mention a few of his accomplishments;
> **Mark Farner** – Lead singer and guitar for the 70's monster band, Grand Funk Railway
> **Randy Bachman** – Lead member of two number-one groups, The Guess Who and Bachman Turner Overdrive
> **Felix Cavaliere** – Keyboard and singer for The Rascals, the number-one rock band in the world from 1965-70

He said the magic words: "Money is no object." So I told him we'd work it out.

Ringo's son Zak Starkey our drummer had another project, so I made some calls and got hold of Liberty DeVitto, Billy Joel's drummer, and Mark Rivera (one of the truly great saxophonists who played with Billy Joel, Hall & Oates, Peter Gabriel, Simon & Garfunkel, John Lennon, and Billy Ocean among others) to fill out the band and we were off to the races. I got all of them together and discussed the terms. It would be a favored nations structure (everybody got paid the same) first-class travel and accommodation etc. They were ecstatic so the deal was made.

We met in Minneapolis on an agreed date for rehearsal and then left on a private jet for Vancouver for the initial concert. At the end of the show, we returned to our private jet and were advised that we were returning to Minneapolis before leaving for the next leg of the tour, Winnipeg. It was at this point we were told that the hubs had not yet been established in any of the six cities, so we would be unable to travel from one city to the other. Accordingly, after every performance, we would board our private jet, fly back to Minneapolis, and then leave Minneapolis on a designated flight to the next city. We were unable to travel between any of the two cities, no matter how short the distance. Not unlike the system employed by FedEx. So when we finished in Toronto, rather than flying a couple of hundred miles to Ottawa, we would fly 690 miles to Minneapolis and then turn around and fly 890 Miles to Ottawa. The guys weren't pleased, but I said, "It's not me. It's the client. You're getting top dollars, private jet and per diem, so smile." And they did.

At the end of the tour, Randy and I had to fly from Halifax to Minneapolis to come back home to Vancouver. Others, to Minneapolis to get back to Nashville, L.A., or wherever they were living at the time. But as they say, that's show business.

Now not to pat myself on the back, although I don't mind doing that, but just to point out the difference between a manager, and a successful manager, at the end of the tour, I got hold of Mark Begelman, president of Office Depot as well as the Mars Music Group. He had licensed Randy's hit, "Takin' Care of Business" for several million dollars and was getting ready to open a huge chain of Mars Music Stores across the country. I told him "You're opening stores across the country. You need the Mar's All-Star band to tour the cities and promote the new stores." He loved it and I got hold of the guys and we did a second, hugely successful tour, only without the huge air miles this time, just all the money and perks.

It's all about taking care of business.

47

A CHECKERED PAST

Part of acquiring collectibles is accessibility. But equally important is some basic knowledge of what you're dealing with. A prime example was my experience with the great Chubby Checker, one of only two artists ever to have the same song peak twice at number one on Billboard.

I was looking after the entertainment programs at the PNE in Vancouver with different artists every night. On the day Chubby Checker was the headliner, he and his tour manager arrived, and I showed them to their dressing room. After they settled in, Chubby's tour manager inquired about sound and lighting checks, catering, and other matters that he was concerned with, and I put all his concerns to rest. Then I addressed certain of my own concerns.

I have an extremely large record collection of almost all the artists in the business. When it comes to Chubby Checker's records, I had most of his 45s that had been released on the Cameo Parkway label. I had acquired these when I became aware that because of internal legal disputes at the label, most of the records were no longer available, including his massive hit of *The Twist*. Re-recordings were always available, but copies of the original releases were few and far between. Over the years I had managed to assemble several copies of each, complete with their picture sleeves. So after resolving Chubby's tour manager's issues, I told him I had several album sleeves I'd like to get autographed by Chubby and as well, that my girlfriend who was there, was a dancer, and I'd like to bring her on stage when Chubby called for a volunteer to do the twist with him. He said that wouldn't be a problem.

It was an hour before the time for the performance and I hadn't heard back from the tour manager, so I found him outside of Chubby's dressing room and said, "Excuse me. I'd like to get Chubby to sign some things." He said, "Now's not the time. Maybe after the show." Then he said, "I've got to go to the box office. Keep an eye on Chubby in case he needs anything." He knocked on the door and when Chubby opened it, he told him he was going to check the box office. I stepped up and said, "Hi. Just to let you know, if you need anything, there's a phone in your room. Just dial 113. It's my direct line in my production office. Anything you need, call. If I need you for anything, what do you want me to do?" Chubby said, "Just knock on my door."

I got a security guy with a golf cart to take the tour manager to the box office, waited a couple of minutes, knowing it would take him around half an hour to get to the box office and back, and then knocked on Chubby's dressing room door. I said, "I'm sorry to disturb you again. I've got a bag here with some of your records. I wonder if you'd mind signing them for me." He said, "No problem. Come on in."

I went in and laid out numerous 45s in their picture sleeves on the table. He looked at them and said, "Hey, that's me." I said, "It sure is." He said, "They're all different." I said, "Have you ever seen these?" He said, "I've heard about them and might have seen one or two but not as many as these. Are these yours or for fans?" "I said, "No they're all mine. I'm a big fan." He said, "Great. I'll sign them. What would you like me to put on them?" I figured leave well enough alone, so I said, "Whatever you'd like to say would be great."

He started doing that, and while he was signing them, I pulled several of the duplicates I had with me out of my bag and said, "I have some duplicates of these, and I'd like you to have them." And I gave them to him. A huge grin spread across his face. At that moment, I heard the golf cart coming back with the tour manager and I figured I could be in trouble. Fifteen minutes to show time and I'm standing there with my records spread out on the table. The door opened and the tour manager walked in and asked what was going on. I said, "I'm a collector and Chubby was kind enough to sign some records for me."

Chubby said, "Look at this. He's got almost every single I issued." The tour manager said, "Okay, but you've got to go." Chubby said, "Wait a second. I haven't finished. These 45s are on Parkway. My old label with my name and picture. And he brought some for me as well." I figured it was time to make my exit, so I said, "Have a great show Chubby." The tour manager turned to me and said, "Are you finished? Can I get a word in edgewise?" Chubby looked at him and said, "This was a highlight for me. Having a fan with me while you were away and then getting these old 45s." He turned to me and said, "Thank you."

It was obvious the tour manager's nose was a little out of joint, as he said to me, "Okay. It's 5 minutes to showtime. How about you walk Chubby and me to the stage? Then you go on about your business. Five minutes before the show ends, you'll wait, bring us back here, and then walk us out to our car. And that's it."

I smiled and turned to Chubby and said, "No problem. But before we go, my girlfriend is here. I'd love to have her on the side of the stage with me. She's a great dancer. When it's time for you to do the twist, you can call her out and she'll do it with you. I promise you won't be disappointed." The tour manager said to Chubby, "Don't you usually choose someone from the audience?" I said, "Guys, she's gorgeous and a great dancer. You'll love her." Chubby said, "Done. Say no more. We've got our dancer."

The show was great. My girlfriend danced, and everybody was ecstatic. I took them back to the dressing room after the show and waited. When they were ready, I took them to where their car was parked and then turned to Chubby and said, "That was a great show. Thanks for coming. Before you leave, would you mind if I took a couple of pictures?" (I had a friend there with a camera). The tour manager said, "We've got to go." Chubby turned to him and said, "You get in the car and stay in the car. I'll be there shortly." Then he took a bunch of pictures with me and with my girlfriend. In all fairness, I have to say that his tour manager was just doing his job, but I was incredibly grateful that Chubby was such a nice man and so generous with his time. A true gentleman. The kind of man who was totally deserving of all the success he enjoyed over the years.

48

In Other Words

We have all said things we wished we could take back. Congratulating a woman on being pregnant when she wasn't. Meeting an old friend and asking, "How's that beautiful wife of yours?" only to find out she ran off with his best friend. It's all part of the human experience. But sometimes, we are just innocent bystanders.

It was the early eighties and Anne Murray was in Vancouver and I had been hired as production manager for her show. She had her own group of professionals, road and stage manager, techs, the workers. I wasn't one of her people, just handling the production of the show. I had to be there to observe what was going on and make sure there were no problems.

During all the sound and lighting checks, the stage manager said, "Let's hear from the lighting guy. He's up there with the spotlights and he's got some concerns." Their lighting guy was up above the balcony, 200 feet from the stage, but they were all connected by microphones. Then the stage manager turned to Anne Murray and said, "The lighting guy wants to talk to you about some of the lighting." Anne said, "Where is he?" and the stage manager pointed to the balcony and said, "He's up there." She looked but couldn't see him, so the stage manager talked to the lighting guy and said, "Turn off some of the lights. Don't blind her. She'll answer anything you want. Okay, you can talk to Anne now, she's here." He handed her the microphone and said, "Anne, it's Roger from the lighting company."

Now you must understand that normally there's very little communication between the techs and the artists. Mostly the techs deal with the stage manager so she's not familiar with the techs, but in this case, it was one-on-one. The lighting company was from Montreal and the lighting guy was French Canadian. So when the stage manager said he could talk to Anne, he said, "Anne, do you want to focus?" But being French Canadian, he has a strong accent, and it comes across as "Do you want to fahkus?" Anne gave the stage manager a dirty look and he came running over and she said, "Just exactly what did he ask me?" The stage manager shouted out for everybody to quiet down, and they stopped fooling around with their guitars and drums and he said, "Roger, would you repeat what you want Anne to do?" Roger said, "I'll ask again. Anne, do you want to fahkus?" Anne looked at the stage manager and said, "I don't want any part of this." and stormed off, rattled.

Now the lighting guy was of course merely trying to get Anne to focus. He needed to adjust the spotlight for color combinations and direction so that during her performance he could follow her with the spotlight without blinding her. He just wanted her to focus on the spotlight so he could adjust it, but unfortunately, as Paul Newman said in *Hud*, "What we've got here is a failure to communicate"

Misunderstandings weren't always vocal. When I was hired as production manager for ZZ Top, prior to the show, their manager came over to me and asked for a favor. They were planning on shooting a video the day after the show for their hit "Legs" and he wanted 20 or 30 attractive young women to appear in it. He asked if I wouldn't mind going out during the performance and approaching attractive women with invitations to the video shoot which, if they were willing to come, also contained a release that they would have to sign. I agreed and during the first act of the show, I went out into the crowd with a couple of guys from security and approached around a hundred women with the invitations.

The next day I walked into my production office and my secretary said, "You're famous." I asked, "How am I famous?" and she said, "You made the paper." and handed me a copy. I read the article, which talked about the show and how great it was, and then went on to say that during ZZ Top's performance, a bearded man was seen going through the audience looking for bearded clams. What she failed to mention was that some of the guys in the office had changed the report, which should have read: "During the performance a bearded man was seen going through the audience looking for attractive women and inviting them to an opportunity to be in a video shoot for 'Legs' the next day." The guys had photocopied it and doctored it to read what I had looked at. I was incensed and grabbed a phone and called the local paper asking for the editor. When he got on the line and I was about to read the riot act, my secretary started giggling and told me what the guys had done. I thanked the editor for the nice article and of course felt really stupid.

But sometimes what was set out in black and white was actually set out in black and white.

The story goes that a man meets a fellow on the train going to work one day. The fellow is down in the dumps and when he asks him what's wrong, the fellow says "I really screwed up. My wife and I were going to Pittsburgh to visit friends. When we got to the station, there was a woman selling tickets who was well-built and wearing a low-cut top. I meant to say, "Two tickets to Pittsburgh, but instead, I said, 'Two pickets to Tittsburgh' and now my wife won't talk to me."

The man looks at the other fellow and then says "That's not so bad. The other day at breakfast with my wife, I was eating and reading the paper, and then I meant to say, "Would you pass me the cream?" Instead, I said, "You cow. You've ruined my life."

I was producing a show for the great Gene Pitney. His manager came to me and asked for suggestions for a playlist for Gene's show that I thought would play well in that city. I told him that everybody in the city knew and loved Gene and that whatever he did would be great, but I sat down and prepared a playlist which Pitney followed, and the crowd loved him. It was a huge success.

After the show, his manager asked me if I could get him a copy of the early reviews to read the next morning on their way to the airport. I went out early, picked up the papers, and checked the reviews. They gave a great review, but the headline was "Titney Scores Big." Discretion is the better part of valor, so when I drove them to the airport, I advised him that the paper wasn't out yet, but I'd send it to him. One of the few times I didn't follow through on a promise. I was just grateful that the show had been held at a local theater and not at one of the larger restaurants in town, Mother Tucker's.

49

WHAT'S UP, DOC?

There may have been more than two doctors in rock and roll, but the only two that come to mind are Dr. John and Dr. Hook and I got to work with both. As I sit down to write this chapter, it's been seven months since Ray Sawyer a/k/a Dr. Hook passed away and seven days since Malcolm (Mac) John Rebennack Jr. a/k/a Dr. John joined him.

When I heard a few days ago that Dr. John had died, the last thing that crossed my mind were stories about the time I spent with him. In the music business, when someone you've worked with passes away, you are more likely than not to remember all the things about them and their performances than you are about your relationship with them.

Dr. John was a giant of a man and a composite of all the great musicians who came from Louisiana, the birthplace of the blues. Dr. John was born in New Orleans in 1941 and began his career as a professional musician at age 13. He sang, composed, and played guitar and keyboards, and his music combined blues, pop, jazz, boogie-woogie, and rock and roll. He won six Grammy Awards, appeared as himself in half a dozen films, and wrote and performed the score for the film version of John Steinbeck's *Cannery Row*. He battled addiction until in 1989 he completed his final rehabilitation and remained clean the rest of his life.

I met Dr. John in 1989 when he was part of the initial *Ringo Starr and His All-Starr Band Tour*. Unlike the 1995 show when I was the road manager, I was just the production manager in 1989. Mac was the ultimate character in wild jackets and feathers, a great singer with that bluesy kind of voice. When he sang his trademark "Iko Iko," he would stand while he played the piano and when the other band members joined in, he'd push the piano fifteen feet across the stage with his stomach, doing his trademark movements. Incredible showmanship. Just a lovely man.

What I remember about that performance, other than Dr. John, are two things. Firstly, in addition to Ringo, the lineup also included Nils Lofgren and Clarence Clemons of the E Street Band, Joe Walsh of the Eagles, Rick Danko and Levon Helm of The Band, and Jim Keltner. Talk about all-stars. And yes, Bruce Springsteen did make an appearance as a guest star that year on the tour. Secondly, that was the only time in my career that I can remember three world-class drummers performing on stage together at the same time, Ringo, Levon Helm, and Jim Keltner. For those of you who may not be familiar with Jim Keltner, he was characterized as the leading session drummer in America, having worked on solo sessions with three members of the Beatles, as well as with Carly Simon, the Bee Gees, Bob Dylan, Randy Newman, Steely Dan, J.J.Cale, Roy Orbison, Pink Floyd, Neil Young, Sheryl Crowe, CSNY, Simon and Garfunkel, Jerry Lee Lewis, John Mayer, and Boz Scaggs to name just a few. To see those three playing drums together was like watching The Three Tenors sing. Something you'll never forget.

I had two tours with Dr. Hook. The first involved half a dozen performances and was called for reasons I've never known, the *Bag the Snake Tour,* and was uneventful. The second tour was a *Super Seventies Tour* in the 90's involving thirty-plus shows, with Dr. Hook as the opening act followed in order by Rare Earth, Grand Funk, The Guess Who, and finally Bachman Turner Overdrive.

The only matter of consequence happened early in the tour. Half an hour before showtime, one of the guitar players came to tell me that Ray Sawyer wasn't prepared to open as only 500 people had arrived so far, even though the performance was sold out, and he wanted to trade places with one of the later acts. I told him to come with me to my temporary office and had him call the band's manager. I got on the phone, told the manager what the guitar player had told me, and then told him that it wasn't a problem. The band could go home, they would be replaced the next day and there would be no money. Then I handed the phone back to the guitar player. He listened for about a minute while there was screaming on the other end of the line and then hung up and told me they would go ahead and open.

I mentioned the above merely to illustrate the world of a road/ tour manager. You get your artists and their equipment to the venue, ensure their dressing rooms, schedule, riders, catering, sound, lights, merchandise, etc. are all in order, and then settle financially with the box office before the end of the night. The other small part of being a tour/

road manager is taking care of six-year-olds. Which is probably why I never had children.

But what I must tell you of interest about Dr. Hook is that despite what everybody assumed, Ray Sawyer was not Dr. Hook. After Dennis Lecorriere left the band, Ray became the lead singer and throughout the band's history, as a dozen members came and went, he was the constant. But Dr. Hook was the name of the band and was inspired by the fact that Ray Sawyer had lost his right eye in a near-fatal car crash in Oregon in 1967, after which he always wore an eyepatch. When Sawyer left the band, he toured as Ray Sawyer of Dr. Hook. When anyone asked the guys in the band which one of them was Dr. Hook, they generally directed them to the bus driver.

In the music business as with everything else in life, things are not always as they seem to be.

50

TRIBUTE IS THE HIGHEST PRAISE

Audio and video recordings of artists ensure that their music lives on with us long after they're gone. But for their devoted fans, often that just isn't enough. This explains why tribute artists remain one of the most symbolic and symptomatic evidentiary proof of the immortality of music. The artists may be gone, but for those who loved them, they're just not prepared to let them go.

For the past couple of decades, in addition to occasionally looking after touring artists, I have been concentrating on being the road and tour manager for my friend Les Vogt and his partner Wayne Webb's great tribute bands as they tour across the continent. I mentioned Les earlier but permit me to give you a little more background on one of the truly great impresarios of rock and roll.

Les began as the lead singer of a local band, The Prowlers. During his career, he shared the stage with such greats as Bill Haley, Gene Vincent, Eddie Cochran, Roy Orbison, and Jerry Lee Lewis. Les's record "The Blamers" knocked Elvis Presley's "It's Now or Never" off the # 1 position on local stations and remained #1 for 11 weeks. Les was the producer of the first international tribute show, *The Legends of Rock and Roll*, followed by *Elvis, Elvis, Elvis.* He remains generally regarded as the king of tribute bands covering artists like Elvis, Roy Orbison, Buddy Holly, Jerry Lee Lewis, and Jackie Wilson.

Les's story doesn't stop there, however. Les was a concert promoter for such greats as James Brown, Jerry Lee Lewis, Tina Turner, and Roy Orbison. He owned a recording studio, operated several nightclubs, was a successful booking agent, and managed Roy Orbison. Roy was leery of New York and Los Angeles managers whom he didn't trust, but I remember once when he told Les "You're the only one I trust to manage me." Les also created and produced *This Lonely Heart,* a musical story of the life of Roy Orbison which still tours worldwide. I'm proud to say Les is my friend.

For the past six years in the course of my duties as road and tour manager for the tribute bands, I was followed around by a film crew for The Documentary Channel who recorded hundreds of hours of material which were ultimately reduced to an 84-minute film called *Almost, Almost Famous* which at some point has or will make its way to a theater in your city. It's a behind-the-scenes look at the tribute artist industry, which, as defined by *The Hollywood Reporter*, "is a rotating-membership affair run by Marty Kramer, a veteran tour manager who has worked in the biz for 54 years." For me, as for so many others, these tribute bands help keep the music alive. Although I could share hundreds of stories with you about life on the road with tribute bands, I shall limit myself to just two.

The first involves Roy Orbison. As I mentioned, Les managed Roy during the latter part of Roy's career and was both a great friend and admirer of Roy's talents. Several years after the tragic death of Roy's first wife Claudette, Roy met and fell in love with Barbara Jakobs while touring in England and they married and remained together and devoted to one another until his death. Which in the great confluence we know as life brings us to Larry Joseph Gulbransen, or as he came to be known, Larry Branson.

Larry was born on the West Coast, one of five children of second-generation Norwegian/Canadian parents. Larry's father was an amateur musician and with this musical background, Larry had learned to play guitar by age 12. Larry left school after grade 10 to work in his father's painting business. During this time, his uncle who had a great talent for impersonation taught Larry some of the vocal skills which ultimately stood him in good stead as he changed career paths.

Following his career as a painter, Larry went to work in electronics, although his passion remained with music. His major impediment was his shyness, however, and he never imagined he would have the confidence to perform in public.

In 1968, fate intervened. A workmate had a small four-piece band, and they needed a manager. Although he would have preferred to play guitar, he agreed to accept the position. As it turned out, they were all instrumentalists with no vocalist. After listening to their version of "Pretty Woman," Larry suggested he join on vocals and so, on that first time he performed with a band, the song was the Roy Orbison classic. Larry joined the band as a vocalist and stayed with them for 5 years. He then went on to a solo career and from 1973 to 1988, his popularity grew.

Once again enter Lady Karma. Over a period of four years, Larry was doing regular gigs at a hotel called the Coach House. Larry had become friendly with the manager of the hotel, who was also a friend of Les Vogt. At that time, Les was Roy Orbison's Road manager and he had booked Roy and Barbara into the hotel overnight while they were performing elsewhere. Larry performed several of Roy's songs in his act and the hotel manager thought it would be good for Roy to hear him and arranged for them to come to the show. Unfortunately, nerves overcame Larry and there was no way he could bring himself to perform any of Roy's songs in front of him, so the opportunity passed.

Fast forward 10 years to 1988. Larry heard that Roy had passed away and was deeply saddened. After mulling on it for a while, Larry contacted Les with the idea of doing a Roy Orbison tribute. A week later, Les let Larry know he would be coming out to see him perform and would be bringing some guests. His guests were Roy's brother Sam Orbison, Red Robinson, actor, producer, singer, and songwriter Alan Thicke (and father of Robin Thicke), Margaret Trudeau (Prime Minister Pierre Trudeau's wife), and me. We had wanted Sam to see Larry as we wanted the show to be *Sam Orbison presents A Tribute to Roy Orbison,* so we needed him to sign off on Larry. I was watching Sam during the show and while Larry was singing, I saw tears rolling down Sam's cheeks. After the show, we all went backstage. Sam introduced himself to Larry and told him how he used to travel with Roy and look after the sale of merchandise and then he said to Larry "I just buried my brother and watching you, you are my brother." We all agreed we would meet again the next day. The next day we met at Les's office and Sam said, "I'm in." and so the *Legends of Rock and Roll* was born. Les decided that instead of just Larry as Roy, we should have some of Roy's friends, so the show consisted of tributes not only to Roy but to Elvis and Buddy Holly as well.

It was a few years later and John Mueller who was one of the great Buddy Holly impersonators partnered with Les Vogt to do a European tour of Roy and Buddy, featuring Larry Branson as Roy and John as Buddy. We had our own production manager, and I was the tour manager. We were running short of merchandise so I asked our local promoter Mark Howes if he could help us, and he said we should come down to his dad's office and he was sure he could get us what we needed. As it turned out, his father was Arthur Howes, one of England's great promoters and a charming man. I recalled he served us tea and Eccles cakes, which is of no importance other than I'd never had Eccles cakes before and got addicted to them. I noticed Mark's father had a poster hanging on the wall of an early 60's concert in which Roy Orbison was the featured act and the Beatles were the opening act. I mentioned to Mark that a blow-up of the poster would be great as a backdrop on either side of the stage when the guys performed, and he agreed. He took the poster to his printer, got it blown up, and put it on two big pieces of cloth and we hung it on each side of the stage before every show. Also, before leaving for Europe, Red Robinson had put together a slide projection show of every song on the set list so that as Larry performed each of Roy's songs, Roy Orbison singing that song would be projected onto a large screen overhead. The crowd loved it, and I should point out that we sold out the London Palladium at roughly $125 U.S. a seat, something never done before by a tribute artist. Mark also managed to get us a huge supply of CDs from a local rack jobber which satisfied our needs.

Following this, Larry went on to perform for five years in Europe in *Only the Lonely*, a musical tribute to Roy, and then in Les's musical tribute to Roy, *This Lonely Heart*.

So why am I telling you all of this? The answer is simple. It exemplifies everything about the music tribute industry that determines its success. There are literally thousands of talented musicians who can impersonate every great artist, but there are only a few who can do it in a manner that the audience will feel they are reliving the past with the original artist rather than just an impersonator. Les's talent has been in finding those one or two who can sing, talk, and move exactly like the original. We're talking about people like Shawn Klush, Ted Torres, or Donny Edwards who played Elvis, or Lance Lipinsky who impersonates Jerry Lee Lewis, or Zachary Stevenson and John Mueller, both of whom brilliantly impersonate Buddy Holly. And when it comes to Roy Orbison, Larry Branson is the best. Which brings me to the rest of that story.

It was early in the 2000's and a group of filmmakers had decided to make a movie, *The Roy Orbison Story* and they had found the perfect man to play Roy, namely Larry Branson. They approached Barbra Orbison for the rights to do so and arranged to take her to see Larry perform. Which was when everything went off the rails. Although totally onside with the project, once she saw Larry perform, she withdrew her consent. She maintained it would just be too haunting. She said that Larry wasn't just a good Roy impersonator, on stage he became Roy. He sang, moved, and became Roy to such an extent that she couldn't distinguish one from the other and it was just too much for her to have to bear.

I fully understood Barbara's decision, but I always regretted it. Roy's life was the quintessential rock and roll story. Growing up in a small Texas town, getting a guitar from his father at age 6 and deciding he was going to be a musician. Playing in a Medicine Show at age 10. Meeting Johnny Cash and being referred to Sam Phillips and Sun Studios, touring with Sonny James, Johnny Horton, Johnny Cash, and Carl Perkins, highs and lows, tragedies and comebacks, friends with the likes of The Beatles, The Rolling Stones, Bob Dylan, Buddy Holly, Elvis, The Beach Boys, Tom Petty, and George Harrison, never succumbing to the scourge of drugs and alcohol, but writing and singing and touring until his early death of a heart attack at age 52, quiet, humble and self-effacing, always polite and considerate, avoiding the spotlight whenever possible. On stage, one of the greatest voices in rock and roll. Once he was off stage, however, he was shy, soft-spoken, and gentle. Generally regarded as the sweetest man in the business.

In one of his last interviews, he was asked how he felt about the adulation he received, and he responded "I don't quite know how to feel when people compliment me and use words like 'legend' or' inspiration' or words like that. But there again, these were just gifts I was given, and I like if I received the gifts, I like to pass them along. Whatever people think of me, I'm grateful. But it's not a lot of my doing. God gave me the voice. Not a lot I had to do with it. God gave me a gift. A very nice gift. I try to thank him quite often." With a few exceptions like Ringo and Bruce Springsteen, the likes of Roy Orbison are few and far between.

My second story involves another of our impersonators who, like Larry was able to become the artist he was impersonating. Only more so. Jackie Wilson was a hugely prominent figure in the world of pop, rhythm and blues, soul, and rock and roll and was one of the most important and influential musical artists of his generation. His live shows inspired

James Brown. Michael Jackson and Elvis Presley as well as numerous other artists that followed. He and Presley were good friends. Wilson was sometimes called "The Black Elvis" and reportedly when asked about this, Presley said, "I guess that makes me the white Jackie Wilson." What almost nobody outside of Jackie's family is aware of however is what happened in September 1975 when Jackie suffered a massive heart attack and stopped breathing. He was taken to a local hospital and resuscitated but had suffered brain damage resulting in his floating in and out of consciousness. He was basically incapacitated for the rest of his life. He was also financially destitute. When Elvis heard about this, he said, "Don't worry. I love you man. I'll pay for everything, which he did, doctors, hospital bills, prescriptions, everything, until he died. And even though Elvis died years before Jackie finally passed, Elvis had ensured that his estate would look after Jackie as long as he was on the planet.

Berry Gordy wrote in his autobiography *To Be Loved* that Jackie Wilson was "the greatest singer I've ever heard." Because of the fervor, incredible dance moves, singing, and wardrobe he brought to his performances, Wilson was dubbed "Mr. Excitement," a title he kept for the remainder of his career. He was named #69 on *Rolling Stone's* 100 Greatest Artists of All Time. Which brings us to Bobby Brooks.

Bobby Brooks was our Jackie Wilson impersonator in our *Class of '59 Legends Tour*, along with Lance Lipinsky as Jerry Lee Lewis and Ted Torres as Elvis. But Bobby's story goes back a little further. Bobby was born in New York state but somehow ended up in South Carolina in their foster system. He had a difficult childhood, with an array of childhood diseases that would have traumatized the strongest of individuals. While still a teenager, he joined the U.S. Navy where he spent the next ten years until he was honorably discharged. Shortly after separating from the Navy, Bobby made a decision that would change his life forever and decided to participate in a talent show, performing the James Ingram ballad, "Just Once." This led to other public performances until Bobby was approached by Peter Hernandez to join the Hernandez Family group, which included Hernandez's then-six-year-old son Peter Jr., who would ultimately emerge as Bruno Mars.

After watching Bobby perform one evening at a show in Hawaii in 1994, Paul Revere of Paul Revere and The Raiders approached him and asked him to do a Jackie Wilson medley, insisting that Bobby had all of Jackie Wilson's moves and vocal talent. Bobby declined, maintaining that he was a performer, not an impersonator. Revere persisted however and approached John Stuart of the Las Vegas-based *Legends in Concert* tribute shows, who hired Bobby to perform, although not at first as a Jackie Wilson impressionist. A little later, Bobby was performing at Bally's in Atlantic City portraying Jackie Wilson during a run of the *Legends in Concert* show when one evening the iconic Motown vocal group the Four Tops decided to check him out. After the show, they met with Bobby and one of the group pointed out the incredible similarities between Bobby and Jackie Wilson, their voices, moves, and even their laughs, and he insisted that there had to be a genetic relationship. This led to meetings with some of Jackie's children and an ultimate DNA test which proved that Bobby Brooks was indeed Bobby Brooks Wilson, the son of Jackie Wilson and Bobby's mother who was 14 when she had known Jackie Wilson.

The music never dies because one way or another, neither do the stars.

7
ODDS AND ENDS

51

BITS AND PIECES

Silent Songs, Brief Conversations

I produced a show with Julio Iglesias. He arrived at the theater with his assistant early in the afternoon to do all his prep. He instructed his assistant to do all the things I would do when one of my artists was performing, sound checks, light checks, batteries, etc. His guy went for lunch, out for a smoke, and forgot to check the batteries. That evening, Iglesias was announced and walked out to the cheers of the crowd. He picked up the mic and began to sing, but no sound came out. He looked at the crowd and then over to his sound guy at the side of the stage who was panicking. Iglesias walked calmly to the side of the stage and handed the mic to his assistant, who was standing beside me, and said, "Not working." His guy handed him another mic and said, "Working." Iglesias took the mic and said, "Not anymore. You're fired."

Walking the Plank

One of the perks of managing tours and producing shows is you get to go head-to-head with major stars and live to talk about it. I was producing a series of shows for Billy Idol. Mid-tour, we were listening to a version of "Shaking All Over." He said it was a great version, but not as good as the original version by The Who. I replied that the original wasn't by The Who, it was by Johnny Kidd and The Pirates. I had the single, and Chad Allan who was with the original Guess Who heard it, and then they recorded it. I told him I had the test pressing and record. Billy said, "We'll see about that." When we arrived at our show in Vancouver, I went to my home, got the records, and went to his dressing room with them and said, "As I promised." He said, "You're right, I'm wrong." Mind you, I haven't been on his Christmas list since then, so perhaps not a major victory.

One Door Closes, Another Opens

It was 1983 and The Beach Boys were in town. They called and asked if we wanted to come to the show at BC Place, a dome with a retractable inflated roof. We said absolutely and went to the theater to find they had a special guests area set aside called "The Sandbox." There was food, drinks, girls in bikinis and half a dozen chairs. Halfway through the show, they announced that Burton Cummings was in the audience and invited him on stage to perform with them. Burton went on stage and together they did a killer version of "Barbara Ann."

After the show, we went backstage for a meet and greet after which we all left together as our limos were in the same place behind the arena. The exit to the parking area had an airlock, which meant that the door into the room had to be closed before the door to the parking lot was opened or it would collapse the roof. We all walked into the room, but Dennis Wilson was a little slower. The security guard had just closed the door as Dennis rushed to get in, and he smashed face-first into the door. I saw what had happened and called for them not to open the door to the outside and we went back outside the room to where Dennis was lying semi-conscious on the floor bleeding from his nose. We got him first aid and then proceeded on our way. Just another day at the beach.

You've Got Mail

It was 2009 and I was in L.A. having lunch. There was a fellow sitting next to me wearing a lab coat of some kind. As I have a habit to do, I chatted him up and said something like "Always enjoy lunch more when I have a doctor sitting next to me in case anything goes wrong." He said, "I'm not a doctor, I'm a med student." I asked, "Where are you working now?" and he answered, "I'm working assisting the Chief Coroner on the Michael Jackson autopsy." Of course, my next question was "What can you tell me?" He replied, "Absolutely nothing." I gave him my card and said, "Well, if anything comes up you can share, see what you can do. Send me something."

Two or three months later, an unmarked envelope comes to my office. The Michael Jackson Autopsy report. My only regret is that I never had a chance to have lunch next to the guy who did Donald Trump's tax returns.

*Sitar*day is Traditionally the Jewish Day of Rest

Because of my relationship with Ringo Starr, I was asked to be the production manager for a performance by Ravi Shankar taking place at a local theater. Shankar was the brilliant Indian musician who helped popularize the harp-like instrument known as a sitar. He was also a close friend and collaborator with George Harrison and the father of Norah Jones.

I produced the show, but unfortunately, never got to see it. It had been an incredibly busy week, working twenty-hour days, not only with Shankar's show but several other commitments as well. As a result, when I arrived at the theater, I was exhausted. We had box seats, so I just sat back and relaxed, and the next thing I knew, it was two hours later and the concert was over. I'd slept through the entire performance.

We went backstage after the performance and I felt I had to say something nice, so I said, "Your performance knocked me out. I was in a special place." He said, "So glad you enjoyed it." "I responded, "I loved every minute of it. If it had been longer, I promise you I would have been out of this world."

Sometimes the Little Things Ain't So Little

It was the fall of 2008 when the great AC/DC rolled into Vancouver as part of their world tour. I was production manager for this stop on their journey and was very much looking forward to their arrival. Shortly before they were expected at the concert site, I was confronted by their manager who was panicking because there weren't any ashtrays in their dressing room. I explained that the local laws prohibited smoking in the dressing rooms and in the building overall. He started to shout about how the band had to smoke as it was part of their show, and they needed to have glass ashtrays. Before their manager could get more excited, I calmed him down and told him I would look after it.

I called around to various stores, but nobody seemed to carry ashtrays anymore. So I got into my car and went to the closest thrift store where I found an assortment of around a hundred glass ashtrays—some advertising beers, some with tourist destinations, and a few celebrating a royal wedding—each selling for $1.29. I picked out a dozen of the best and returned to the venue with my bag of ashtrays. As I walked in the door, the manager was standing there, and before I could say anything, AC/DC walked in the door behind me.

Before either myself or their manager could say anything, lead guitarist Angus Young looked at the "No Smoking" sign on the wall and said, "What the fuck is that about? We're smoking. Are there ashtrays in our dressing rooms?"

Their manager started sputtering about local laws, but I stepped in and said, "No problem. I have your ashtrays right here. Let me show you to your dressing room."

I led them to their dressing room, which was right beside my production office, and Angus said, "Come on in." Their manager started to say, "He's just the production manager..." but Angus gave him a dirty look, put his arm over my shoulder, and led me into the dressing room. I spread out the ashtrays and they were thrilled with them, loving the wide variety.

Then Angus said, "What about on stage?" Part of Angus's routine involves him smoking on stage and then parking the lit cigarette on the tip of one of the guitar strings. "Not to worry," I said. "You just do your show. I'll take care of it." I placed ashtrays everywhere on stage and the show went off without a hitch. The guys were terrific, and I had a great time with them.

So what's my point? It's simple. Many people think that much of rock 'n' roll is smoke and mirrors, but sometimes it's just smoke and ashtrays.

That's Bordering on Expensive

Most of my tours were international in character which meant crossing back and forth across the U.S.-Canadian border. Normally this didn't present a problem other than:

a. When working as a non-resident you are required to obtain a work visa ahead of time to permit you to do so; and
b. When they have a criminal record.

As tour, road, or production manager, I would deal with the work visa issue on a regular basis as it was generally my responsibility to ensure that everybody had their necessary documents. When one of the artists had a prior criminal conviction of any kind, however, this was a different matter. Assuming it wasn't a matter of too grievous concern, I was generally able to surmount the problem. Inasmuch as I dealt with the officials on both sides of the border on a regular basis, we had a pretty good working relationship. When it came to certain convictions, however, it was another matter. Both sides of the border were a great deal stricter when it came to drugs. This was just another reason why I assiduously avoided any involvement with drugs whatsoever as I had to ensure that at least I was squeaky clean.

A perfect example of the problem arose when Crosby, Stills and Nash were booked into a concert in Vancouver. I was advised that David Crosby had a prior conviction for things like drugs, firearms, and DUI and was not going to be allowed to cross the border. I was finally able to negotiate a deal whereby I would meet David when he arrived at the airport, then escort him directly to the venue for the concert, stay with him, and then after the concert bring him back to the airport. There would be no hotel or overnight stay, or any other diversions. In support of this, the company was required to post a $25,000 bond which would be forfeited if there was any breach.

Fortunately, David was both appreciative and cooperative and everything went according to schedule. After the concert, I escorted him back to the airport and anxiously awaited the departure of his plane.

One of my favorite movies was the 1960 classic, *The Magnificent Seven* with Yul Brynner, Steve McQueen, and Charles Bronson. At one point, Steve McQueen who plays a gunfighter named Vin Tanner is asked why he returned to defend some villagers who had betrayed him, and his friends and he says something to the effect of, "I had this friend. One day we were riding through the desert, and he stopped, got off his horse, took off all his clothes, and began to roll in the cactus. And when I asked him why he did it, he just said, 'It seemed like a good idea at the time.'" I've never been a gambler. Never had the time or the inclination. So looking back, perhaps taking a $25,000 gamble wasn't the smartest move, but at the time, it seemed like a good idea.

Where There's Smoke……

It was 1995 and we were in Tokyo for the Budokan stop on the Ringo Starr and his All-Starr band tour. I learned that Harry Connick Jr. was performing a late show in the city, so after our concert, Zak Starkey, John Entwistle, Billy Preston, Mark Farner, Felix Cavaliere, and I went over to see him perform. After the intermission, we returned to our seats and the lights went down, but no Harry Connick Jr. We waited and waited and then Harry came running down the aisle out of breath and went on stage. After the show, we went backstage to see Harry and found out what had happened. The building was a no-smoking facility, so during the intermission, Harry stepped out back behind the theater to smoke a cigarette. As it turned out, when he tried to get back in, the stage door to the theater had been locked and Harry had been unable to convince any of the security guards that he was entitled to enter. He then went out front but having neither a ticket nor any money with him, wasn't allowed into the theater. He finally managed to convince one of the attendants at the door that he was the show by pointing to a poster and they allowed him in. Sometimes smoking can be hazardous to more than just the second act of your life.

Reach For the Top

I believe I would be remiss if I didn't give a shout-out to one of the great bands of all time and their manager.

For fifty years, ZZ Top have played a large role in the music world, with the same band members from day one, Billy Gibbons, Dusty Hill, and Frank Beard. With record sales of more than 50 million albums, including *Eliminator,* which sold more than 10 million copies in the U.S. alone, ZZ Top has been one of the best-selling most popular touring bands ever.

I had the pleasure of working with the band on numerous occasions, and on the last occasion, I was approached by their manager Bill Ham to make it a permanent gig. The band was getting ready to leave for a year-long worldwide tour. They had just lost their road manager and Bill asked if I would like to take on the position. I was very flattered and told him I'd have to get back to him as I had made a tentative commitment to one of my artists. I called my artist to check on his plans and he told me he was planning on starting a six-month tour in sixty days and needed me. Reluctantly I called Bill, thanked him again but explained that I had made a commitment and felt I had to keep my word. He understood but it was always something I regretted having to do, as I'm satisfied that one-year engagement would have extended well beyond, and I believe that because of the relationship I had developed with the band members, when Bill ultimately retired, I might have had the opportunity to take over management. Regardless, I've never been a big fan of second-guessing and what it is, and I'm just grateful for the times I got to work with the guys and for the fact that Bill Ham, one of the business's great managers, producers, and impresarios was kind enough to have offered me the position.

Bill passed away a few years ago at the age of 79 at his home in Austin. Bill had shaped the band's image, co-written several of their songs, produced their albums, and managed them for more than 25 years so I have no doubt that as far as Billy, Dusty, and Frank are concerned, he remains the fourth unnamed member of the band.

Hey, Hey We're the Monkees

For those of you who might not remember, The Monkees were a band consisting of Micky Dolenz, Michael Nesmith, Davy Jones, and Peter Tork that were put together for a TV show in the 60s and then went on to record and tour from 1966 to 1971 and sporadically for numerous years later. There are many, including *Rolling Stone* who claim that the band never received the recognition they deserved, and considering that they sold over 75 million records and in 1967, according to the *Washington Post,* they sold 35 million records, more than the Beatles and The Rolling Stones combined, there is merit to that claim.

Part of the disrespect arose from the rumor that supposedly, the band didn't always do all their own instrumentation and possibly did some lip-synching. This was around the time of the big MIlli Vanilli lip-synching controversy. I can't tell you one way or another with any authority, but I was working on one of their earlier concerts and there was a problem at the start of the show. There was a sound guy at the side of the stage who had a large tape player with reel-to-reel tapes. When the band was ready to go on, the DJ/announcer said, "Ladies and gentlemen, the Monkees" which was the sound guy's cue to start the tape playing, whether for vocal or instrumental, I'm not sure. The Monkees came on stage but unfortunately, the sound guy had failed to properly affix the safety clamp that held the reel in place, so when he pushed play, the reel went flying off the machine and rolling across the floor. I sent the DJ/announcer back on stage to say there would be a short delay and the band would be right back. The guy scampered after the reel, rolled it up and shortly thereafter the show started again, and everything was fine.

I next worked with the band several years later when my friend David Fishoff booked them for a reunion tour. We were in Nashville and after the show, the promoters said they needed a picture of the Monkees so I went and got them. There were only three of them as Michael Nesmith wasn't there, and they insisted there should be four, so I was conscripted to be the fourth Monkee as seen in the picture opposite. Hey hey, I'm a Monkee.

52

I BELIEVE IT'S STARTING TO SNOW

As I mentioned earlier, I've limited any discussion in the book about drug use, even though you've heard that the music world is rife with it. The explanation is simple. If you hope to succeed in my line of work, you'd better be prepared to abide by our form of Hippocratic oath, which is "See nothing, say nothing" (i.e., What happens in Vegas, stays in Vegas").

Cocaine is generally the drug of choice in the music world, and it's called snow, or more correctly, most people use the Yiddish word for snow which is shnay. Now truth be told, I encountered more shnay during my career than you'd ever see in a snowstorm in Alaska in January. I saw guys snorting shnay of women's bare breasts, off the back of their hands, off glass tables, and off toilet seats. One of my clients used to travel with a box of Dristan inhalers for stuffed noses, except his inhalers all had a mixture of cocaine. Drugs and booze never held any attraction for me, since in my line of work you must have your wits about you 24/7. Most emergency calls came for me in the middle of the night rather than during the day and I couldn't afford to have my senses dulled if I wanted to stay in the business.

In fairness to musicians, you must understand the nature of their lives. They work incredibly long hours, often at unusual times of the day and night. And they party just as hard. Performing on stage for several hours, musicians can lose several pounds and end up totally exhausted. They are constantly surrounded by people who want pieces of them, whether it's their professional advisers or assistants or their audiences, they have little private life, and often drugs are their only high. I'm not trying to justify it, just to explain it. Shnay is often to musicians what watching television or having a martini is to the general public. But truth be told, it's a pain in the ass for those of us concerned with the general welfare of the artists and ensuring the shows run on time. There have been more concerts than I care to think about that have been derailed by a shnaystorm.

53

HIT THE ROAD, JACK

I believe that one of the main reasons I was well respected by the artists with whom I worked, whether as a road, tour, or concert production manager, was that I never placed any boundaries on my responsibilities, or what I could do to help them in any way possible. The best example that comes to mind relates to perhaps one of the greatest artists of modern times, the legendary Billy Joel.

It was 1993 and Billy was playing the Pacific Colosseum in Vancouver. I was the concert production manager for Perryscope Productions who were presenting Billy, and in the course of conversations with Billy's tour manager Max Loubiere, unrelated to the concert itself, I learned that Billy had been unsuccessful in his efforts to locate a white Land Rover he wanted to buy for his wife, Christie Brinkley. Apparently, there was a year-long wait list everywhere in the U.S.

I mentioned to Max that I might be able to locate one in Vancouver, made a few calls, and sure enough shortly thereafter I located a dealer who had one he was prepared to sell. While Billy was doing his sound checks,

Max and I went to the dealership, closed the transaction, and arranged to have the car delivered backstage to the Colosseum. Before Billy went on stage, Max surprised him with the car which only left the problem of how to get it back to New York.

The tour had a tour bus and a truck that carried all their merchandise and miscellaneous equipment. We transferred enough of the merchandise and equipment to the bus storage space, loaded the Land Rover onto the back of the truck, and problem solved. Max was Billy's tour manager for 30 years and was brilliant at his job. Like me, he understood that a tour manager's job wasn't just getting your artist to and from the engagement, but anticipating their needs, and solving the problems that were thought to be insolvable. I was pleased to make a fellow tour manager's life a little easier.

Sing me a song, you're the piano man
Even though I may not be a star
I know I can't croon, or carry a tune
Still, I'm the guy who found you that car.

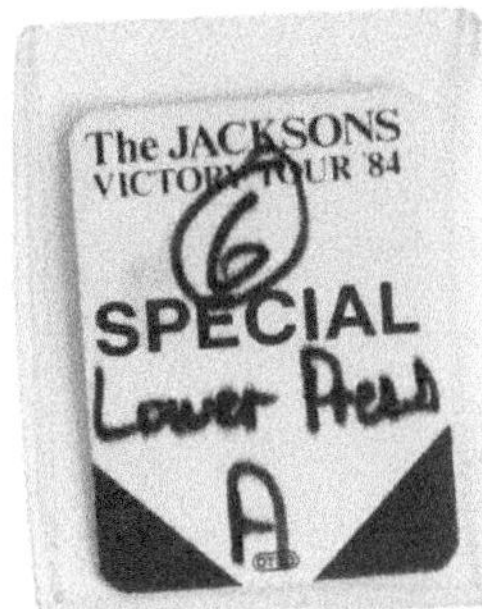

8

YES, VIRGINIA,

THERE MAY BE NO SANTA CLAUS BUT THERE IS LIFE AFTER ROCK AND ROLL

54

DID SHE MENTION MY NAME?

I believe that the reasons music has played such an essential ingredient in people's lives over the millennia are twofold:

1. Nothing can express the emotional swings of our lives better than music; and
2. By expressing these emotions through music rather than viscerally, whether it's joy, grief, love, jealousy, rage, despair, celebration, lamentation, success, failure, or whatever, it's cathartic and generally prevents any of these events from imploding our lives.

I believe the greatest songs are those that deal with love found and lost since those are some of the most impactful and often devastating events in our lives. Songs such as George Jones, "He Stopped Loving Her Today," Kris Kristofferson's "Loving Her Was Easier Than Anything I'll Ever Do Again," Prince's 'When Doves Cry," the Beatles' "Hey Jude," Whitney Houston's "I Will Always Love You," and The Righteous Brothers' "You've Lost That Loving Feeling." For whatever reason, my favorite has always been Gordon Lightfoot's wistful, nostalgic ballad, "Did She Mention My Name."

It's so nice to meet an old friend and pass the time of day
And talk about the hometown a million miles away
Is the ice still in the river? Are the old folks still the same?
And by the way, did she mention my name?

The scene is the upper floor of a professional building. Two marriage counselors are waiting for the elevator at the end of the day. One turns to the other and says, "I don't know how much longer I can do this. Every day it's the same thing. The same complaints. He doesn't communicate. She doesn't appreciate him. He's tired all the time. She's busy with the kids. All he does is work. All she does is spend. Every day it's the same thing, just different people. I've got to be honest. I don't know how much longer I can go on listening to these people complain. How do you do it?"

His friend looks at him and says, "Who listens?"

As you probably know, marriages in the music industry are generally short-lived, with many, many artists having many, many marriages. Forget about those who have been married only twice. Frank Sinatra was married four times, Jerry Lee Lewis, seven times, Jennifer Lopez four times. Willie Nelson four times, Liza Minnelli four times, David Foster five times, Kenny Rogers five times, to name just a few.

It's not that surprising. Long days on the road, working weekends and evenings, generally being surrounded by people in a celebratory mood and wanting to party. Not the ingredients for fidelity and longevity as far as relationships are concerned. I believe the only other workplace with similar divorce statistics is probably the hospitality industry since, except for the long days on the road, all the other ingredients are there.

Did she mention my name just in passing?
And when the morning came, do you remember if she dropped a name or two?
Is the home team still on fire? Do they still win all their games?
And by the way, did she mention my name?

It seems I've been on the road for much of the past fifty years. For all practical purposes, I left the city where I grew up when I was still a young man, moving to the East Coast and then the West Coast, but mostly just traveling from city to city with one artist or another, and never in one place for very long. I decided very early on that the profession I'd chosen wasn't exactly suited for long-term relationships and so, with certain regrets, I moved on.

I have no doubt that if I sat down with Freud for about 90 seconds he could diagnose why "Did She Mention My Name" is my song of choice, and I'm not oblivious to the reasons. I've never been one to live in the past or to second guess my life decisions. I love the work I do and that I've done all my life and know that had I chosen to pursue a relationship, it would have ended with my wife and any children disengaging themselves from me at some point in time. So I have remained single all my life.

I will admit that when I get together with old friends and their wives and talk turns to their homes, children, and grandchildren, my mind does wander and I sometimes think, *What if?*

Did she mention my name just in passing?
And looking at the rain, do you remember if she dropped a name or two?
Won't you say hello from someone? There'll be no need to explain
And by the way, did she mention my name?

55

THE WORLD'S OLDEST TALENT AGENCY

Although the term "busking" only goes back to the middle 1860s in Great Britain, buskers or performers working in public places for gratuities have been an integral part of world culture dating back to antiquity. Most of the world's greatest artists will acknowledge that at some time or another, they were a member of the busker community. One of my better-known artists once told me that there was no such thing as a part-time musician if you wanted to be a success. You either gave it your all or forgot about it. This meant there were usually many lean years where you would struggle just to put food on the table.

Joan Baez, Woody Guthrie, B.B. King, Janis Joplin, Bob Dylan, Jimi Hendrix, George Michael, Tracy Chapman, the Grateful Dead… different times, different genres, but all of them at one point or another, were buskers. One of my favorite performers, Passenger's brilliant Michael David Rosenberg, best known for his ballad "Let Her Go" left school at age 16 to become a busker in England and Australia. Even though he continues to perform to sell-out crowds, he can still often be seen going back to his roots, busking on the street. (You can see him perform "Rolling Stone" on the street on YouTube). He summed it up best for I believe most buskers when he said, "All of my stagecraft is something you need to learn. Busking is what taught me. Taught me a lot about people. You're spending most of your life in a city center, watching people and interacting with people. When you're a busker, you tend to attract the weird and the wonderful. All those experiences were great in allowing me to grow as a person, a songwriter, and as a performer."

David and I have been fortunate to have spent most of our working years with some of the world's greatest artists. As we get older, there's a tendency to want to give back so for the past year, we've been working with a local busker, Shawn Bullshields. Shawn came to the world of busking late in life. After a greatly disadvantaged youth, he'd been working as a private contractor in the construction industry and suffered an injury that restricted his doing heavy lifting. His wife suggested he should try busking, so he applied to Vancouver's tourist destination, Granville Island which attracts several million visitors a year. He was immediately accepted and has been performing there daily for the past eight years, other than when he is appearing at concerts or festivals in Western Canada. With a lilting voice somewhere between Gordon Lightfoot and Eddie Vedder and a presence that immediately attracts crowds, accompanied only by his acoustic guitar, Shawn quickly became Granville Island's most popular busker, and his reputation continues to grow.

Shawn and David recently composed a song that I believe sums up much of the life of your average busker. It's called "The Balladeer."

You'll see him out there on the street playing his guitar
He'll strum some chords and then repeat
He ain't no kind of star
You may hum along and tap your shoe
Not like you've better things to do
And when he sings you find your smile appears
Cause he's the balladeer.

He'll make you smile and stop a while
To listen to his song
He'll do his show then move along
It's not like he's done something wrong
He ain't no star like Richard Gere
He's just a balladeer.

And all the while he plays and sings
The women smile and think of things
His soft voice brings to mind

The love they'd hoped to find
There were a lot he'd come to know
Who'd stay behind after the show
Now he's just one more memory
The balladeer's a man who must be free.

He'll make you smile and stop a while
To listen to his song
He's got these stories he can tell
And a changing message he can sell
But he ain't no Bill Shakespeare
He's just a balladeer

So gather round and gather near
There's lots of room and friendship here
And love this roving balladeer will share
And maybe if your spirits lift
You'll leave a monetary gift
So others can enjoy what he can spare.
There're people waiting for him everywhere.

He's got no fancy beach house by the sea
Nor any daily grind like you and me
His home's the road or where he stops
His truck is often where he flops
He ain't no Leonard Cohen or even near
He's just a balladeer.

He'll make you smile and stop a while
To listen to his song
He can make time slow
While he does his show
And sometimes even make it disappear
Cause he's the balladeer

Sadly, you can have all the talent in the world but that may not be enough. Sometimes, the gods of music must smile on you as well. As I write this chapter, Shawn has just returned from Nashville where he received a standing ovation when he opened for Tim McGraw at a fund-raising benefit before a large crowd, including no doubt many of the industry greats. It's what I love about the world of music. Sometimes there's another great story, just around the bend.

56

A ROSE BY ANY OTHER NAME

Over the past 60 years, we have both been privileged to meet and work with some of the world's greatest artists. And it has indeed been an honor. Having said that however, we both agree that perhaps the greatest benefit we've derived from our chosen journey as we traverse this incredible adventure we call life has been, when out of nowhere, because of our respective pasts, we cross paths with someone whom in a hundred years we never would have anticipated we might meet. And yet perhaps as the perfect example of the adage: "Man plans and God laughs," things don't always turn out as expected.

A short time ago we met and became friends with someone whom we both believed might be one of the great performance artists today. She was a beautiful young woman by the lovely name of Bulelwa Mkutukana, better known by her stage name, Zahara, which translates to 'blooming flower'. Although we were unable to agree as to whom her incredible voice recalled, the closest we were able to come with was somewhere between Tracy Chapman and Edith Piaf. It was a powerful vibrato that owned every song she performed, just as she owned every stage she stood on, whether in front of an audience of a hundred or ten thousand cheering enthusiasts. Her music has been roughly categorized as "Afro-soul" and she sang in her native language, Xhosa, as well as in English. Quite simply, she was not just a great singer, she was a great artist. She was also a champion for women who were victims of violence.

If you haven't heard of Zahara, it's because she was only now venturing into North America. She was one of the best-selling artists in South Africa, had six great albums, her debut album sold out in 72 hours, and within 17 days reached double platinum status in South Africa, with a similar reception for her following albums. She received accolades such as Best Female Artist, was a judge on *Idol's South Africa*, and was invited to perform a bedside concert for the great Nelson Mandela in his home, who called her his daughter.

We were working with Zahara on what was to be her first English language album for release in North America to be followed by a North American tour in 2024. We hugged Zahara just before she returned to her beloved South Africa to perform a major concert and planned on meeting again at Christmas. Then two weeks before Christmas, Zahara passed away at the so early age of 36 while waiting for a liver transplant.

Now here's the thing that impressed both of us even more than her great talent. We both agreed that if we possessed even an iota of Zahara's artistry, we would probably be stopping everybody we met and asking them "Do you know who I am? Have you heard what an incredible singer I am?" And yet Zahara was one of the most unassuming, gentle, kind, gregarious, friendly, and downright lovely people either of us have ever had the good fortune to know.

So pay attention. You never know when a new flower may be blooming in the music garden, although you are unlikely to come across a more spectacular one than Zahara at any time soon.

Zahara's signature song was "Ndiza" in which she sang "I will come, I will come back." No need Zahara. You never left. You will always be here in the hearts of all South Africans and most certainly in ours. For purely selfish reasons, we are directing part of the proceeds of this book to the Nelson Mandela Foundation in Zahara's name, so that every time we think about or see this book or every time the book is read, it will be our way of saying "We love you, we miss you, and you will always be on our mind"

57

CAPTIVE AUDIENCES

Over the years, I've found that some of the most appreciative audiences for my bands hadn't paid a penny for their tickets.

Back before the formation of The Guess Who, I managed a band called the Devrons, which included Burton Cummings. I had booked the band into Marymount School, which was a wonderful institution operated by The Sisters of the Good Shepherd to house and assist pregnant girls and women who had nowhere else to go. As we were the city's most popular band with slews of young girls always following us, I thought that in addition to being goodwill, a visit to the school would be more beneficial to the members of the band than a lecture on the wisdom of contraceptives might be.

We were well received by the residents of the school, with a little rock and roll music being a nice break from their rather staid and challenging day-to-day existence. As we were leaving, the nuns approached to thank me and told me that they would pray for me, which I greatly appreciated. I may be Jewish, but I've always tried wherever possible to cover all the bases.

A short time thereafter, I booked the band into a concert at the Headingley Correctional Institute. This facility accommodates some 500 inmates serving sentences of two years or less. Once again, we were well received, with standing ovations. After the concert, the warden assigned six inmates to help us load our equipment into our van. Once everything was loaded, I went to thank the inmates for their help, but could only find five. I asked about the other one but received no response.

I opened the back of our van and saw all our equipment. There was also a large box which held all our drums. I lifted the lid and tucked in with the drums was number six, a slight young man. I thanked him for what was his obvious intention of going with us to help unload the equipment but said we'd be fine and suggested it would be best if he rejoined his friends. Which he did.

Several years later, Bachman Turner Overdrive was asked to perform at the Prince Albert Penitentiary. This is a much different facility than Headingly since it also houses around 500 inmates, but many of those were serving substantially longer sentences for much more serious crimes.

We performed our set, and the audience gave us a standing ovation and refused to sit down. We left the stage and the warden approached us and said we should do an encore. I pointed out that we had done all 13 songs in our set and were out of time. He responded by saying that at Prince Albert you were never out of time unless you were paroled or died, and the crowd was getting out of control, and we should get the hell back on stage. I huddled with the guys and told them to go back out and perform the Animals hit, *We Gotta Get out of This Place* which they did. And were met by an even louder reception as they left the stage, and the inmates were shouting and screaming for more. I took Fred Turner, our lead singer aside and told him what he had to do. He went back on stage with the band and told the crowd that the band was finished, but he was going to sing one more song for them, one which they rarely did. He sang *Jail House Rock*. The inmates went wild, the band left the stage, and we got the hell out of there as fast as we could.

One more captive audience I'd like to mention. It was early 1999, and I received a call from the U.S. Air Force asking if Randy Bachman's band would headline a concert at the upcoming closing of Howard Air Force Base in Panama. I have several cardinal rules, but right near the top is that you never pass up an opportunity to perform for the troops, so I grabbed the chance.

We flew from New York City and were met by a representative of the Air Force who then transported us to the Howard base which was six miles southwest of Balboa at the Southern end of the Panama Canal. We got settled in the guest barracks and then I proceeded with Randy to do our usual setup and sound checks. Once this was completed, we still had three hours until the concert and the young officer accompanying us asked if Randy and I would like to see the Stealth bombers. We had no idea that they were even located on the base but immediately accepted. They were housed in a totally camouflaged facility which from the air could never even be identified as a hangar. Of course, we were told that no pictures were allowed, but we were shown the planes up close, and then one of the pilots who had been watching the sound checks asked if we'd like to go for a ride with him in the bomber as they were leaving for surveillance flights. Regrettably, there was no way we could be guaranteed we would return in time for the concert, so we had to decline. As we headed back to the performance area, we heard a giant "whoosh" and all you could see was a blur as the bombers took off. Then we got a tour of the rest of the base and a couple of aircraft carriers they were loading all their equipment on in preparation for vacating the base.

The concert went off without a hitch. The band performed all their hits, and the troops were incredibly enthusiastic, singing along with "Takin' Care of Business," "You Aint Seen Nothing Yet," "Let It Ride," "Lookin' Out For #1," "Roll On Down The Highway," all of them. It was just a great night.

We were there for two days and ate most of our meals with the troops, but before we left, the base's commanding General insisted on taking Randy and me out for dinner to a fine dining establishment in Panama City. The meal was fabulous, the General and his wife were charming and gracious and couldn't have been nicer or more welcoming. And the General's wife presented us with t-shirts titled "Rocking the Ditch March 27th, 1999" specially prepared for the band by A T & T who provided communications for the base.

If my parents hadn't been so poor, it's entirely possible that I would have gone to university and law school and become a wealthy lawyer, putting vicious criminals back on the streets or fighting heated custody battles to deprive one of the parents of their visitation rights. Instead, I got to entertain the troops, participate in the closing ceremonies of a major Air Force base, have dinner with a General and his wife, and inspect and be offered a ride in a Stealth bomber. Also, I get to sleep nights. God bless rock and roll.

58

Where Were You On...?

I'm not sure if you'd call it karma, irony, destiny, coincidence, or none of these. For me, it was the worst day of my life.

I was in New York City with The Guess Who. We were on a 32-city sold-out tour across North America with the great Joe Cocker opening for us. We had come from a show in Erie, Pennsylvania with the next show scheduled for Holmdel, New Jersey on September 12th. Our crew were staying in Secaucus, New Jersey and the band and I were at the Times Square Sheraton in Manhattan. Our two tour buses could unload in New

York but weren't allowed by the Port Authority to park there which is why they were staying in Secaucus.

We arrived on the night of the 10th and I and several of the band had gone to a club to see the legendary Les Paul. The following morning, shortly after nine, I got a phone call from Bill Wallace, the band bassist who asked, "Do you have the TV on? A plane just flew into a building here." I turned on the TV and saw the initial report of the plane flying into the World Trade Center.

I immediately called Sam Boyd who was with the crew in Secaucus. He was planning on taking the shuttle into New York that morning with the crew for breakfast at the World Trade Center. I told him to sit tight. Then I called the band's manager and each of the other members of the band to let them know the situation and that the concert on the 12th would obviously be canceled and they should just wait for me to get back to them. Shortly thereafter Bill Wallace called me back and said he was planning on going for a walk and I agreed to join him in the lobby in twenty minutes.

When I got down to the lobby, there was mayhem. There were several hundred people milling around and an abundance of security personnel checking identities. Bill said, "Let's hit the streets." We left the hotel and for reasons I really can't explain, we decided to head towards the World Trade Center some four miles away. Looking back, I can only describe the next five hours as a crazy melange of thoughts and visual impressions:

As we walked, there was this continual buzzing of helicopters as they headed toward the World Trade Center.

- Next, we heard this tremendous noise which turned out to be crowds of thousands of people coming towards us. We were the only idiots headed in the other direction.
- On the sidewalks, owners of restaurants, coffee shops, and other stores had set up tables with various muffins, pastries, sandwiches, coffee, and juices they were offering to people fleeing the scene. Not selling, giving them away in a spirit that can only be described as New Yorkers standing up for one another.
- Fire trucks. Ambulances and police cars with sirens blaring were all passing by us heading towards the World Trade Center. More and more we had the feeling we were in the middle of a war zone.
- As we got closer, we saw tow trucks bringing out cars, buses, and trucks still smoldering and dropping them on side streets and heading back.

- People were running everywhere.
- As we got closer to the World Trade Center, we saw cars covered with burnt shreds of paper and soot. When we were about five blocks away, we saw this cloud of smoke and dust that seemed to be descending on where we were heading. It looked not unlike the mushroom cloud you see when they show a nuclear explosion. We had no idea at that time of the extent of the damage, the loss of life, or the fact that it was a terrorist attack but decided that we couldn't go further into that horrible doomsday scenario and quickly reversed course and headed back to the hotel.
- Shortly after arriving back at the hotel, Burton Cummings and I walked down to Times Square. It was unbelievable. Totally empty, save for one pretzel vendor. Other than that, nobody. No cars, no people. Nothing. Burton and I bought
- pretzels and sat on the curb watching the giant screen in Times Square broadcasting CNN. I can only describe it as surreal.
- The rest of the day was spent watching events unfold on TV and learning of the extent of the carnage.

The next morning, my head shifted into tour manager mode, and I began to make plans on how to get my people out of New York. We had another concert scheduled for Boston on the 14th, so I had to be concerned with getting the band to Secaucus and on their way. The problem was that there were no buses, cabs, or vans leaving the city. You could get out, but then you weren't allowed to come back, so none of the commercial vehicles were interested in driving us. The situation in the city was almost riotous. Tourists were anxious to get out of the city with none of the normal for-hire transit willing to drive them. No planes flying and no cabs, vans, or buses leaving the city. It was like a scene from the movie Escape From New York.

I called an old friend Mike Reda for help. I had known Mike for 30 years. He was a cab driver in New York and one of the world's biggest Guess Who fans. He and his brother Frank would come to our concerts everywhere and had a huge collection of our memorabilia. Mike offered to come and get us and drive us to Secaucus in his personal Cadillac, but that wouldn't work. There were too many of us, the band, their wives or girlfriends, the manager plus their luggage and several guitars. We needed some kind of bus. Mike said he would get back to me. Shortly thereafter,

Mike called to let me know that his boss owned a livery company that also operated in New Jersey. One of the New Jersey buses had come into the city for servicing, oil, lube, and filter changes and the driver who brought it in was ready to head back. We agreed to pay $1,000 and that was that. The following morning, the 13th, the driver picked us all up at the hotel and we were gone.

The bus arrived at the crew's hotel in Secaucus, and we had an emotional greeting from the crew. I've never admitted this to anyone before, but I got off the bus, walked around to the back of the bus opened the door to unload our luggage, and then looked back towards New York and saw the smoke still rising. I got down on my hands and knees and kissed the ground. We still didn't know how many individuals working in or visiting the buildings had lost their lives, or how many of the incredibly brave first responders had perished rushing to help them. What I did know was that there are no rules and no guarantees as to how many days we're allowed on this side of the turf, and we should be grateful for every single one granted to us.

A few final thoughts.

Our friends and families all knew we were staying at the Sheraton in New York but didn't know if it was the Times Square Sheraton or the one near the World Trade Center which burnt and collapsed after the attack. For the following week, a great deal of my time was spent on the phone fielding calls from concerned friends and family. I didn't have a phone plan and my monthly long-distance charges were normally in the $200 range. For September 2001, they were $1500.

If I had decided to book us into the Sheraton near the World Trade Center rather than near Times Square, or if the crew had decided on an earlier breakfast at the World Trade Center and I had joined them, I would imagine I might not be writing this book.

And one last corporeal and less spiritual thought. As I mentioned, we had two tour buses, one for the crew, and one for the band. Each bus had limited space. It had sleeping provisions for 12, one shower, a kitchen, a meeting area, and seating for the daytime. There was one small bathroom, but it was only for washing up or urination. Other bodily functions were verboten, so you looked after that before boarding the bus, or else we had to stop at gas stations or restaurants along the way. Everybody's stomachs were greatly out of order from the previous couple of days so needless to say, for the next few days we made an awful lot of stops.

Looking back, I've been blessed to be privy to and part of fifty-seven years of the last century's most joyful music, and I need every second of it to sublimate the incredible sadness of that September day.

59

SUNRISE AND SOMERSET

W. Somerset Maugham was an early 20th-century English writer of plays, novels, and short stories. One of his tales concerned Albert, a verger at St. Peter's, Neville Square who had worked hard as a church official for 16 years, and then is fired when the new Vicar discovers Albert can neither read nor write. Rather than going home, Albert is wandering the streets, dispirited, and he finds himself in a strange neighborhood. He attempts to find a shop where he can buy some cigarettes. But is unable to find one and, realizing an opportunity, decides to open a smoke shop. It becomes hugely successful, so he embarks on searches of other neighborhoods lacking in a similar service and ultimately ends up rich and successful. He opens a bank account which continues to grow and one day the bank manager calls Albert in and suggests that he should be investing his money. During the conversation, the manager learns that Albert can neither read nor write, and he asks what he thinks he would have been if only he could read and write. Albert responds, the verger at St. Peter's, Neville Square.

Recently I attended a screening in my hometown of a documentary about my work with tribute bands titled *Almost, Almost, Famous.* While there, I was interviewed by the press and I was asked how a poor orphan from a small midwestern town ended up thousands of miles away, intricately involved with some of the greatest musical artists of the twentieth century. The thought that immediately came to my mind was "My sister's parents couldn't afford a washer and dryer."

As I said, I was an orphan, and as far as I knew, an only child. Two years ago I learned that in fact, I had two sisters. I still have no idea of the identity of one of my sisters, but I know the other one and have known her most of my life. A few years ago she decided to try and learn more about her heritage and was able to determine that she had a brother and a sister who were with her in the orphanage before she was adopted. Following up on this, she learned of my identity and contacted me. Coming from a small community it wasn't totally surprising that we had grown up only a block or so from one another. She was a little older than me, so although we weren't friends, I knew her and saw her most days when going to or from school. Ultimately, when she grew up, she married one of the sons of a close family friend.

On my recent trip back home, I went to visit her, and we got to talking. She told me that her adoptive parents had told her that at the time she was adopted, they had thought about adopting two children, a boy and a girl, and seriously considered adopting me as well as her. Ultimately however, they decided against it, as they were relatively poor and didn't own a washing machine or a dryer and felt that a young girl and an infant boy would just be too much work for them, and unfair to the little girl, so they only adopted her. I was adopted around two years later, but my parents were poor and remained poor. As a result, when I finished grade ten, I dropped out of school and went to work to help our family financially. Most of my friends went on to university and became doctors, lawyers, accountants, or engineers.

My sister mentioned that finances had substantially improved for her parents as she was growing up and they had sent her to university. Had they adopted me, she had no doubt I also would have gone on to university and become a doctor or lawyer rather than what had ultimately transpired.

I suppose that's possible, but with all deference to Maugham I have always subscribed to what John Lennon said in his song "All You Need Is Love" — "There's nowhere you can be that isn't where you're meant to be."

60

CURTAIN CALL

After 50 years, I decided it was time to leave the road. I was having lunch with David, my friend since the beginning, and as usual, one item or another in the news sparked my imagination, and I began to tell a story about my days with that individual. David pointed out that we weren't getting any younger, and that it was time to memorialize these stories and so for the next year we sat down once a week, I related one story or another to David and ultimately it ended up as this book.

Once this was done, we both decided that despite more than 50 years in the business, we were still too young to retire, so we formed M & D Entertainment Consultants Inc., www.legalandartistinc.com, and we've since been going on to continue doing what we do best. We have several reality shows for which we just completed the pilots, one on Buskers, the other on collectibles, I am entering my fourth year on the Discovery Channel and Animal Planet series, *Pets & Pickers*, and David just published a book of brilliant short stories, *The Day The Rains Came.*

Although it all started with rock 'n' roll, and I'll always love it, there is more to life, and to quote the legendary Sonny and Cher, the beat goes on.